PUT IT IN
WRITING

PUT IT IN WRITING

77 Letters That Get Results

MARGARET WHITE

A**CHOICE**BOOK

PUT IT IN WRITING

77 Letters That Get Results

First published in 1994 by Choice Books, a division of the Australian
Consumers' Association,
57 Carrington Road, Marrickville NSW 2204
Reprinted 1994 (twice), 1995, 1996, 1997
Copyright © Margaret White 1994

Printed in Australia by Australian Print Group

National Library of Australia
Cataloguing-in-publication data:

White, Margaret, 1954-
Put it in writing

Includes index.
ISBN 0 947277 12 9

1. Letter-writing - Handbooks, manuals, etc. Consumer protection -
Australia. I. Title

CONTENTS

6. Professionals 57

7. Neighbours 70

INTRODUCTION

How often do you hear of someone with a legitimate complaint being told to 'put it in writing'? While there may be good reasons for refusing to deal with a problem unless a written complaint is made the requirement discourages many would-be complainants. In the age of the mobile phone and the fax machine, we don't get much practice at letter writing. Having to actually put pen to paper (or fingers to keyboard) can present an insurmountable barrier in the quest for justice.

Put it in Writing aims to demystify the art of letter writing. In Chapter 1, we provide some guidelines for making complaints. By going through 'correct channels' and observing certain proprieties, you will increase your chances of a favourable outcome. You won't have put anyone off-side or unnecessarily on the defensive. You will also have avoided delays caused by directing your complaint to the wrong person.

In Chapter 2, we discuss the basics of letter writing. There are no hard and fast rules when it comes to written communications. There are only conventions and common practices – some of them outdated and unnecessary. Others are worth following because they enhance communication and credibility. Once you are confident about the form your letter should take, you are free to concentrate on the content.

The remaining chapters deal with common areas

of complaint. Each contains a brief outline of the legal position, to let you know where you stand, followed by a selection of sample letters. Two points need to be made: the law in each state and territory is different, so our summaries are very general; and the letters are only samples – don't force your facts to fit.

You may need to get more information about the law as it applies to your problem. We have provided some pointers as to where you might obtain this. Once you are confident that you know your rights, you can use our sample letters to claim them. You don't have to follow the wording of the letters slavishly. There is no one correct way to write a letter. Our letters are merely examples of how a letter might be written in each case to maximise your chances of success.

Letter writing may be old-fashioned, but it is still the most effective means we have of communicating ideas while at the same time creating a permanent, verifiable record of our views. The ability to write a good letter is a valuable asset for the modern consumer.

CHAPTER ONE

MAKING COMPLAINTS

Consumers in today's society have a number of hard won rights – goods must be of merchantable quality and fit for the purpose for which they are sold; services must be provided with care and skill; we are entitled to basic information before we enter into credit contracts; and so on. It is up to us, however, to enforce those rights.

Know Where You Stand

First, it is important to be quite clear about what your rights are. This may not be too difficult if the matter is clear-cut. The following chapters contain information about your rights in different areas and how to enforce them. If you need more information, consult a consumer guide such as *The Complete Consumer – The CHOICE/Investigators practical guide to your consumer rights,* by Jan Bowen and the Australian Consumers' Association, revised edition, ABC Books, 1993. State and territorial consumer affairs departments, community legal centres and regulatory bodies such as the Law Societies and the professional registration boards might also be able to help.

You should be also be aware that the law is constantly changing. While the law in this book was correct as at the time of writing, and the basic principles discussed are unlikely to change much, the details will vary not only from state to state but over time. This is another reason why you should make sure that you know where you stand if your problem cannot be resolved through-initial negotiations.

Know What You Want

Before you complain, consider what it is that you want to achieve. Do you just want to make your point as a matter of principle and perhaps extract an apology? Or do you want money – a refund or compensation for harm you have suffered? Do you want goods replaced or services re-done? Or do you want someone to be rapped over the knuckles to ensure that what happened to you doesn't happen again?

Whatever you want, you should make it clear from the outset.

Act Quickly

If you discover a defect in a product you have bought, or in work which has been done for you, immediately contact the seller, worker or service provider. It is a rule of law that a person who suffers harm must mitigate his or her losses. In other words, you have to do what you can to minimise the harm. Don't drive a faulty car until it completely breaks down – contact the seller straight away so that the defect can be fixed. This rule applies to everything.

You are also more likely to be taken seriously if you complain immediately. And it is more difficult for the person to whom you are complaining to argue that inter-vening factors such as negligent use have contributed to the problem.

Complain to the Right Person

Initially, you should complain to the person with whom you have the problem – the shopkeeper, the profession-al, the contractor concerned – but only if they have some authority to do something about it. If they don't, address your complaint to the manager or whoever is in charge. On the other hand, avoid complaining to someone who is inappropriately senior in an organisation. It will only be redirected, resulting in delays. And when it does finally reach the person concerned, he or she will be offended you did not contact them directly, and won't be disposed to help. If you are not sure to whom you should address your complaint, ring the organisation and find out.

Only if you have tried and failed to get satisfaction yourself should you take your complaint to some outside body, such as a consumer affairs department or a professional registration board.

Put it in Writing

Even if you make your initial complaint in person or over the telephone, you should keep a record of the date and content of the conversation. Make sure you note the name and position of the person to whom you are speaking. Unless the matter is resolved immediately, it is often a good idea to follow up the conversation by sending a letter confirming the details and the fact that it took place.

The telephone, in fact, should be used with caution. There is a good chance that you will have to speak to a junior person and that you will be 'fobbed off' or 'given the run around'. It is also no use trying to obtain information about a product over the telephone. Manufacturers will not usually disclose commercial information on the spot. They might, however, consider your request, and the reasons for it, if you put it in writing.

As a general rule, complaints should always be made in writing, and you should keep a copy of letters you write, as well as any you receive, along with other documents like invoices and receipts.

Stick to the Facts

When you are complaining about someone to someone else, it is important not to defame that person. In order to avoid the possibility of defamation, stick to the facts. Do not express what you are thinking or feeling about that person. For example, 'X promised to investigate my complaint but he has not yet, to my knowledge, done so', is acceptable. 'X is a lazy incompetent who does not keep his promises', is not acceptable. 'The wall erected by Y has developed cracks after only six months', is a statement of fact. 'Y is such an incompetent builder he cannot even build a wall to last more than six months without cracking', may be considered to be defamatory.

Atttacking a person's character makes them less willing to help you.

Take Formal Action

If your own persistent efforts to obtain satisfaction fail, you can take more formal action by taking the matter up with an outside agency. There are numerous bodies who will accept and act on complaints by consumers. These are described in greater detail in the later chapters of this book.

CHAPTER TWO

LETTER WRITING BASICS

'Putting it in writing' has many advantages: you create a permanent record of your communication, which prevents confusion and denials; you can think about what you want to say and check it carefully before sending it; and, for the faint-hearted, it can be easier than actually confronting a person face-to-face or over the telephone.

All of these advantages are lost, however, if your message is not clear and complete.

Remember – the person to whom you are writing cannot use your tone of voice, your facial expressions or your body language to interpret your meaning. Your words must convey it all, and, if you want to get results, they must invite attention and encourage action.

Write promptly, as soon as you have a problem, and *keep a copy of your letter.*

Language

The best letters are simple, straightforward and *short.*

The language shouldn't be familiar, unless you know your reader well, but it does not have to be formal, either – it has to be clear and easy to read. Your letters should sound like you. Don't try to sound like a lawyer unless you are one and don't feel that you have to use words which you wouldn't use in everyday speech.

Avoid expressions like 'for your perusal', 'enclosed herewith' and 'the undersigned', unless you actually want your reader's eyes to glaze over. If you make your letter easy to read, it will be read. An important part of this is language. Redundant expressions and involved sentences obscure meaning. Keep it as short as possible.

Be polite, even if you are very angry. Offending your reader achieves nothing. A simple 'thank you' for reading the letter and considering your request can, on the other hand, have the opposite result. One advantage of letter writing is that you can present yourself as calm and reasonable, regardless of your true feelings.

On the other hand, be direct. Say what you mean and mean what you say.

Good grammar and careful punctuation will make your letter 'flow' well and will help to avoid ambiguities. Don't feel bound by old-fashioned rules, however, unless they actually assist communication.

Format

A neat, attractive letter invites attention. A typed letter is preferable, but remember whether typing or handwriting your letter, always use only one side of the paper.

Your letter should be set out with wide margins, short paragraphs and well-spaced text.

While it is not necessary to slavishly follow 'correct' letter-writing conventions, the basic rules do enhance communication. In short, you should:

- Always include the date, either below your address or in the top left-hand corner.
- Put your address in the top right-hand corner. If you want to be accessible by telephone, your telephone number can be included.
- On the left-hand side, but starting below the bottom line of your address opposite, put the name and address of the person to whom you are writing. By sending the letter to a named person, you reduce the chance that it will be passed around the organisation

and lost or ignored. If you do not know their name and title, (why not call the organisation to find out?), address the letter to 'The Secretary' of a government department, large organisation or association. A letter to a small business may be sent to 'The Manager'.

- Leave some space and commence 'Dear...'. never put 'To whom it may concern'. If you do not know the name of the person to whom you should address your letter, put 'Dear Sir or Madam,'. If you do know their name, 'Dear Mr ..., Mrs ..., Ms ..., Dr ...,' or whatever, is appropriate. Unless you know that a woman prefers to be addressed as 'Mrs' or 'Miss', 'Ms' is probably the best form of address.

- On the line below, and centred, you should, if you can, state what it is that the letter is about. If, for example, you are writing to complain about a defec tive product, you could write 'Re: faulty toaster' or 'Re: Porsche motor vehicle, registration no. ABC123'. If there is an account number or some other reference number that should be quoted, this is as good a place as any to do so.

- Keep your paragraphs short, each one dealing with a single idea. A single sentence or even a single word can constitute a paragraph and, indeed, this can be a very effective method of adding emphasis to an important statement. If you are handwriting your let ter, indent paragraphs, otherwise leave at least one line of space between each paragraph.

- Formal letters should end with either 'Yours faithfully' or 'Yours sincerely'. For the pedants, the former should be used in letters addressed to a 'Dear Sir or Madam', the latter when you have used the person's name.

Content

The purpose of writing a letter is to communicate with your correspondent. You can best do this by putting yourself in his or her shoes. Try to see things as they might see them and let them know that you understand their point of view. Be friendly. Assume that your correspondent is honest, hard-working and fair – at least until you have proof to the contrary.

Your first paragraph must grab the reader's attention and let him or her know exactly what the letter is about. So get straight to the point and preferably keep it to one short sentence.

After that, carefully plan what you want to say, and set it out in logical order. Don't jump around or digress. Thoughts should be clearly grouped in paragraphs. Give your reader all the information he or she needs to make the decision, which you want him or her to make, but no more.

Let your reader know that you know your rights and that you expect them to be respected. If you are unsure, get advice about this before you write. The remaining chapters in this book include details which should help you in this regard. It isn't necessary to quote particular laws. It's enough to say something like, 'I understand that I have a right to ...'.

The final paragraph should also be short – one or two sentences – and should clearly but politely state what it is that you want the reader to do. If you must issue an ultimatum – and they are often counterproductive – make sure that it is fair. If you set a deadline, it should be reasonable and you should be prepared to stick by it. Enclose copies (not originals) of any documents such as bills, quotes, receipts, invoices, statements from witnesses or experts, or photographs of damage which might support your point of view. You did keep these records, didn't you?

And if at first you don't succeed? Be persistent. Write another, stronger letter or take formal action, such as contacting a relevant outside body as noted in Chapter 1.

CHAPTER THREE

FAULTY GOODS

It's disappointing when goods you buy don't turn out to be up to scratch. However, unless you have bought them from an unorthodox seller, such as from a flea market or a garage sale, you do have rights of redress.

Consumer Contracts

Every time you buy something, you enter into a contract with the seller. He or she agrees to supply you with the goods and, in return, you agree to pay the purchase price. In this chapter, we are talking about 'consumer' contracts. Some of the laws which deal with consumer rights define 'consumer' to exclude people who are buying goods or services for business purposes. Thus corporations may be excluded and there may be upper limits on the value of the items purchased. In general, a 'consumer' is an individual who is buying goods or services for his or her personal, domestic or household use.

Contracts are legally enforceable agreements. If one party does not keep his or her side of the bargain, the other is entitled to use the law to obtain a remedy. The two usual remedies are:

- Specific performance. The party at fault can be ordered to fulfil his or her side of the bargain, that is, to supply you with goods as promised. This means you would be entitled to a replacement or to have any defects fixed.
- Damages. If the circumstances are such that the con tract cannot be completed, damages is monetary com

pensation for what you have lost. In other words, you are entitled to ask for your money back.

The contract doesn't have to be in writing to be binding, unless you are buying real estate. It can be entirely oral. But documents such as quotes, invoices, receipts and written guarantees can all be used as evidence of the contents of the contract. For this reason they should be kept. If a problem arises, they'll be very handy. Without such evidence, you still have rights and can enforce them. It will, however, be more difficult.

What's in the Contract?

Your rights depend on the promises that are contained in the contract.

Some of these promises are *expressed*. They are the things that you actually discussed and agreed to. Others are *implied*.

Expressed promises

Obviously, all consumer contracts have a date, a description of the goods and a purchase price. That much is on the receipt. There may also be other matters expressly included, like a written guarantee or promises made by the seller. Sales talk, which is obviously exaggerated, like 'you'll think you're in heaven when you lie on this mattress' does not become part of the contract because no-one would expect such a statement to be binding. Nor are expressions of personal opinion (as opposed to professional) , such as 'I think this is the best sounding CD player around' or 'you look great in that dress'.

If, however, the seller makes statements upon which you could reasonably be expected to rely, such as, 'This car is in really good condition', or, 'This glue will definitely fix your problem', they do become part of the contract. If they later turn out to be untrue, you are entitled to some redress.

Implied promises

Many consumer contracts are, however, entered into without very much discussion between the buyer and the seller. For this reason, the law 'implies' promises into contracts. These implied promises, or warranties as they are called, generally cover the kinds of things which the parties would have agreed to, had they thought about it.

Implied promises were originally part of the judge-made law, or common law, which is developed by the courts on a case by case basis. The Federal Parliament and the state and territorial parliaments have, however, all now passed a great deal of legislation which supplements and, to a large degree, replaces, the common law. Our federal system means that the details of these laws will vary from state to state to territory. There are, however, some basic implied promises which are part of consumer contracts everywhere:

- If the buyer lets the seller know what the goods are wanted for, there is an implied promise that they will be fit for the purpose for which they were sold.

If you tell a shoe salesperson that you want a good pair of shoes for bushwalking and the sole falls off on your first outing, you are entitled to a refund. The shoes were not fit for the purpose for which they were sold. The seller can't turn around and argue that they were only ever intended to be worn for indoor aerobics. If, however, you simply pointed to the shoes and said, 'I'll have a pair of those', you can't complain that they weren't fit for bushwalking because you didn't let the seller know what you wanted them for. You could complain if they were not fit for any purpose (see discussion of merchantable quality).

In the last example, you relied on your own judgement, not the seller's. This particular implied promise will also not be part of your contract if it was not reasonable to rely on the seller's skill and judgement.

If, for example, you asked a sales assistant in a supermarket for something to remove a stain caused by a special type of wood varnish and he or she said 'You could try "Zap", it gets out most things', he or she is obviously not claiming that 'Zap' will do the job. The sales assistant is merely offering a suggestion. It would not be reasonable for you to rely on their skill and judgement in this matter. The case might be different if he or she was an assistant in a specialist woodworking hobby shop and told you that a particular product would do the job.

- Every consumer contract includes an implied promise that the goods will be of merchantable quality. In other words, they must be of reasonable quality, and fit for the purpose for which goods of that kind are usually bought. Kites must fly, clothes must not fall apart when you wear them, CD players should play CDs, and so on.

Goods that are clearly defective are not of merchantable quality. If it is a question of degree, such as how well a kite should fly or how long you should be able to wear a dress before it falls apart, factors such as

13

price are relevant. Obviously, you can expect a better sound from a top-of-the-line CD player than from the 'budget' version you bought in a discount store.

There are two exceptions to the 'merchantable quality' rule. The first is if the seller alerts you to defects, by, for example, labelling them as seconds. They still, however, have to be reasonable quality for seconds.

The second exception is where you have inspected the goods and the defect is one that you should have noticed.

- It is an implied promise that goods are as described. If a table is labelled 'solid timber', you are entitled to expect that it is solid timber and not particle board with a timber veneer. Packaged goods should live up to the picture on the front of the packet.

- If you buy something from a sample, say, carpet for your living room, there is an implied promise that the carpet which is delivered will be the same as the sample.
- It is implied that the seller actually owns, or has the authority to sell whatever it is he or she is selling. If the goods are later confiscated because they were stolen, you can get your money back from the seller (which might be difficult if they are in jail).
- You are entitled to expect that the goods are safe, given their purpose. Obviously, items such as power tools carry inherent risks but they should not have defects which add to these risks.

Written Guarantees

A written statement that something is guaranteed for a

certain time does not displace your rights under the implied terms in your consumer contract. The fact that the time has passed doesn't stop you claiming that the goods were not, say, fit for the purpose or of merchantable quality.

No Refunds

Similarly, a seller can't evade liability under an implied promise by putting up a 'No refunds' or 'No exchange' sign, even if the goods are on sale. You are still entitled to ask for a refund or exchange if the goods are faulty in some way (though not if you change your mind about them or decide that they are the wrong colour or size).

This also applies to signs or written statements that the seller is not liable for faults or defects. This does not apply if goods are sold 'as is' or are marked as 'seconds'.

Manufacturers' Responsibilities

Generally, if goods are faulty, you are entitled to complain to either the seller or the manufacturer. Although you have no contract with the manufacturer, state and federal laws have extended responsibility for faulty goods to the manufacturer. This can be useful if the seller has gone out of business. Of course, you cannot be compensated twice for the same thing.

There are some limits for manufacturers' liability. They are not, of course, responsible for damage which arises after the goods have left their control. More importantly, the laws which make manufacturers responsible for defects are usually aimed at personal, rather than business, shoppers. There may be an upper price limit ($40 000 under the Trade Practices Act) or a requirement that the goods are for personal, domestic or household use.

Manufacturers, however, have some special responsibilities. In particular, they must make sure that reasonable repair facilities and spare parts are available (unless the consumer is told at the time of purchase that these are limited) and they must pay for damage caused by faulty products.

If you suffer significant personal injuries as a result of a defective product, it is probably wise to get legal advice as to how much you should claim before asking for a specific amount from the manufacturer.

Taking Action

As stated above, sometimes you will be entitled to a refund and sometimes you will be entitled to have the goods repaired or replaced. Generally, you can insist on a refund when it would not be reasonable to expect you to accept otherwise. If the item is not fit for the purpose, it is hardly reasonable to expect you to accept another. On the other hand, if the fault is a one-off thing, you would not be entitled to insist on a refund just because the problem has caused you to 'go off' that particular brand.

It is important that you make your claim as soon as possible, particularly if you want to reject the goods.

If your letter does not achieve the desired result, get advice from your state or territory consumer affairs department. You may eventually need to take action in your local equivalent of a consumer claims tribunal or a court.

Letter rejecting faulty goods

Dear   ,
Re: [make and model]

On [date] I bought the above [item] from your shop.
On [date] it developed serious defects.

[Describe problems]

I understand that, as a consumer, I am entitled to expect that the things I buy are of merchantable quality. I am sure you will agree that the [item] I bought was not of reasonable quality, considering the above problems.

I am, therefore, asking you for a refund of the [amount] I paid for the [item][Or to replace the item with another in good working order.]

I trust that this matter can be resolved quickly and look forward to your early reply.

Yours sincerely,

Letter asking for a free repair

Dear   ,

Re: [make and model]

On [date] I bought the above [item] from your shop.
On [date] it developed a serious fault.

[Describe problem]

I understand that, as a consumer, I am entitled to expect
that the things I buy are of merchantable quality. I am
sure that you will agree that, in view of the above problems, the [item] was not of reasonable quality.

While I believe that I am entitled to a refund of the
[amount] that I paid for the [item], I am prepared to
accept a repair of the [item] at no cost to me. If repairs
can be completed quickly and effectively, I will consider
the matter settled.

Please let me know what you propose in relation to
these repairs as soon as possible. I consider 14 days to
be fair under the circumstances,

Yours sincerely,

Letter rejecting goods not fit for the purpose

Dear   ,

Re: [make and model]

On [date] I bought the above [item] from your shop. I had told the shop assistant that I wanted it for [a specific purpose] and he/she recommended the above brand and model.

When I tried to use it for the above purpose, however, [describe problem].

Obviously, the [item] was not fit for the purpose for which it was sold and I am asking you for a refund of the [amount] that I paid for it.

I trust that this matter can be resolved quickly and look forward to your early reply.

Yours sincerely,

Letter rejecting goods that do not match their description

Dear   ,

Re: [make and model]

On [date] I bought the above [item] at a cost of [amount] from you.

When I spoke with your representative on [date], he/she described it to me as [describe]. On that basis, I decided to go ahead with the purchase. I have now discovered that it does not match that description and is [describe goods].

Since the description I was given was the key factor in my decision to buy the [item], the sale was one 'by description'. The fact that the [item] does not fit the description constitutes a breach of the implied warranty that it would.

I have decided, therefore, to reject the [item] and to ask you for a refund of the [amount] that I paid for it. [Alternatively, you could ask them to send you another item that does fit the description.]

I trust that this matter can be quickly settled and look forward to your early reply.

Yours sincerely,

Letter rejecting the seller's denial of liability

Dear   ,

Re: [make and model]

Thank you for your letter dated [date] regarding my claim for a replacement [item][or refund of the price of my faulty item].

Unfortunately, I cannot accept your suggestion that I should complain to the manufacturer.

My contract with you, the seller of the [item], includes, as a matter of law, an implied warranty that the [item] is of merchantable quality. The fact that it is not means that you are in breach of contract. I am, therefore, entitled to expect you to put the matter right.

My claim against you is unaffected by any rights I may have under the manufacturer's guarantee.

I trust that this clarifies the position. Please let me know within 7 days whether you intend to repair or replace the [item] [or give me a refund]. I am sure you will understand that this problem is causing me considerable inconvenience.

Yours sincerely,

Letter to a manufacturer, about damage caused by faulty goods

Dear   ,

Re: [make and model]

On [date] I bought the above item from [name and address of shop]. On [date] it developed a serious fault [describe].

As a result of this defect, considerable damage was done [describe damage, including cost of repairing or replacing whatever was damaged].

As the manufacturer of this product, you have a responsibility to ensure that it is of merchantable quality. You also have a responsibility to pay for damage caused by the fact that it was not of merchantable quality.

I am therefore asking you to replace the [item] with one in good working order and to pay me an amount of [amount] being the cost to me of repairing and replacing the items damaged.

Please let me have your reply within 14 days. I am sure that you will understand that this matter has caused me considerable inconvenience and expense and I am anxious to have it settled as soon as possible.

Yours sincerely,

Letter rejecting goods that are not delivered on time

Dear   ,

Re: [order number]

On [date] I placed the above order for [item] with you. I paid in advance but the [item] has still not been delivered.

It is a term of my agreement with you that the [item] would be delivered within a reasonable time. [Detail any written or verbal promises that were made regarding the time for delivery]. As [period] has now passed since I placed the order, you are in breach of contract.

While I understand that circumstances beyond your control may have contributed to the delay, I cannot wait any longer. If you do not send me the [item] within 7 days, I will consider our contract at an end, as I am legally entitled to do, and will expect you to refund the full purchase price of [amount] to me.

Looking forward to receiving my [item].

Yours sincerely,

Letter rejecting goods not delivered in time for Christmas

Dear ,

Re: [order number]

On [date] I ordered [item] from your Christmas catalogue, enclosing full payment with my order. The [item] was not delivered until [date after Christmas], and I had to buy another [item] from a different supplier before Christmas at a cost of [amount].

It was a term of our agreement that you would supply the [item] in time for Christmas. Having failed to do so, you are in breach of contract. I am, therefore, cancelling the contract and asking you for a refund of [amount], being the full purchase price of [amount] plus [amount] for postage and handling.

I look forward to receiving your cheque within 14 days.

Your goods may be collected from [address] during business hours. Alternately, I will send them back to you on receipt of [amount] for postage.

Yours sincerely,

FAULTY GOODS

Letter rejecting mail-order goods that do not match their description

Dear   ,

Re: [order number]

On [date] I placed the above order for [item] which I had seen in your catalogue. The [item] that I received, however, is not the same as the one in the catalogue.

On page [...], the [item] is described as [quote]. The [item] that I received differs from this and from the picture in the catalogue in the following way [describe differences].

Goods that are sold by description must fit that description. Since the [item] that I received does not fit the description provided in your catalogue you are in breach of your contract with me.

I am, therefore, asking you for a full refund of the [amount] that I paid, which included postage and handling.

I trust that you will deal with this matter quickly and look forward to receiving your cheque.

Yours sincerely,

Letter rejecting mail-order goods damaged in transit

Dear   ,

Re: [order number]

On [date] I ordered [item] from your catalogue. The [item] was delivered on [date] but had been damaged. [describe damage]

As a consumer buying goods by mail order I am entitled to expect that I will receive them in good condition and you have a responsibility to ensure that this occurs. As a reputable business organisation I am sure that you are as disappointed as I am that this problem has arisen.

Please send a replacement [item] as soon as possible. I look forward to receiving it.

Your sincerely,

FAULTY GOODS

Letter complaining about unavailability of spare parts

Dear   ,

Re: [make and model]

On [date] I bought the above [item] from [name and address of shop]. On [date] it broke down and I took it to [name and address of repairer] for repairs. They are included in the list of authorised repairers that came with my [item].

The repairer has told me that the [item] needs a new [name of spare part] and that these are not presently available from you. He says that he has telephoned a number of other authorised repairers and that none of them has the part in stock, either.

As a manufacturer, you will be aware that you have a responsibility to ensure that reasonable repair facilities and spare parts are available. It is not reasonable to expect me to wait indefinitely for a part when my [item] is only [period of time] old.

I am sure that you will understand that this problem is causing me great inconvenience. If you cannot supply the part within seven days I will be forced to claim from you the cost of hiring a replacement [item] until mine can be fixed.

I look forward to your reply,

Yours sincerely,

CHAPTER FOUR

CARS

The implied promises we discussed in Chapter 3 apply to cars, too. The sheer range of problems that consumers experience when buying, repairing, driving, servicing and insuring motor vehicles, however, has resulted in a maze of special legislation. You can get information about your rights in a particular situation from sources such as state motoring bodies, state and territorial consumer affairs departments and industry bodies such as the motor traders' associations.

Warranties

All new cars are sold with a written warranty. The warranty is a promise that any defects which appear within a certain period of time, will be fixed.

State and territorial laws also provide that most used cars sold by dealers must be covered for a specified period of time, depending on the price of the car. Some very cheap cars may not be covered at all. Some defects may also be excluded but this fact has to be noted on a sign in the car's window.

These warranties are in addition to the implied warranties discussed in Chapter 3. The advantage of the written warranty is that defects will usually be fixed without question during the period of the warranty. You can still, however, argue that the vehicle was not of merchantable quality, even if the period has expired.

Whether or not your argument will be accepted by the dealer or manufacturer (or by the court or tribunal if the matter gets that far) will depend on such things as the age and cost of the car and the nature of the fault. You have to concentrate on what is reasonable in the circumstances.

The warranty only applies to manufacturing defects, not to damage done in an accident or through careless driving. As with other goods, if the fault has caused an accident, you can claim damages (compensation) for any loss or injury from the manufacturer. If the amount is substantial, get legal advice before you act. You may also have to decide whether it is better to claim on your insurance and allow them to pursue the manufacturer, or keep your no-claim bonus intact by claiming directly, yourself.

Check when you buy your car whether or not batteries, tyres and other accessories are covered by the warranty. In most states they do not have to be, although you would still be able to claim under the general law if they are not of merchantable quality or fit for the purpose for which they are sold.

It is important to act quickly as soon as you discover a defect, particularly if you want to exercise your rights under the general law to reject the car completely. This would only be possible where you can argue that the car is not of merchantable quality or not fit for the purpose for which you bought it and the problem cannot be rectified by a repair.

Usually, you can get something fixed under a warranty through the dealer from whom you bought it, or from another authorised dealer. If your dealer has gone out of business, however, you can deal directly with the manufacturer or importer.

Cars bought privately or at auction may not be covered by an express warranty but the implied warranties may apply. (See pages 12 to 14).

Repairs

As with all goods, the manufacturer of a car has a responsibility to ensure that reasonable repair facilities and spare parts are available. This applies unless you were told when you bought it that, for example, finding parts may be difficult. What is reasonable will depend, of course, on such things as the age of the car and whether or not it is imported.

As with all service providers, motor vehicle repairers must carry out their work with reasonable care and skill and they must use parts that are reasonably fit for the purpose for which they are intended. (For more on the responsibilities of service providers, see Chapter 5.)

Many problems with repairers arise because the consumer does not know what he or she wants done. Clarify this with the repairer before you leave the car and get a written quote for all but minor matters. Tell the repairer to phone you for authorisation if unexpected repairs are needed which would cost more than say $50. If your instructions are not clear, and you simply leave the car to be 'fixed' or given a 'tune-up' you may have to pay for whatever is done, provided it is reasonable, even though you did not specifically authorise it. In many cases, the 'reasonableness' of the unauthorised work is debatable. You may have to accept a compromise.

If you are not satisfied with the workmanship, the service or the cost of repairs, you should always take the matter up with the repairer straight away and give them the opportunity to rectify the problem. Do not drive your car with a fault because you may do further damage for which the repairer cannot be held responsible.

You can get help negotiating a settlement to a dispute through your motorists' association, motor trader's associ-

ation, consumer affairs department or, in New South
Wales, the Motor Vehicle Repair Disputes Committee.

False and Misleading Statements

If you are encouraged to buy a particular motor vehicle
by a statement or action that later turns out to be untrue,
or misleading, you may be able to obtain compensation
for any loss which you have suffered.

The Trade Practices Act, which is a federal law, contains
a number of sections prohibiting certain kinds of deceptive or misleading conduct, and providing remedies for
consumers. A number of state laws have similar provisions. Examples of deceptive or misleading conduct in
relation to cars might be such things as turning back the
odometer on a second hand car, giving a wrong year of
manufacture or telling a consumer that the vehicle is a
particular model when it is not.

If you think you may have a claim under this type of
law, get advice from your state or territorial department
of consumer affairs, or the Trade Practices Commission.

Letter to a dealer asking for a repair on a new car

Dear   ,

Re: [make, model and registration number of car]

On [date] I bought the above vehicle from you. On [date] it developed serious defects [describe].

The warranty has expired, but I believe that I am still entitled to a free repair because the existence of such a serious defect in a car which has only done [insert number of kilometres] indicates that it was not of merchantable quality when I bought it. This opinion has been confirmed by [independent expert, such as the NRMA, or other motoring association].

Ordinary wear and tear could not account for the problem so soon in the life of the vehicle. I am a careful and conscientious owner as the general condition of the car shows..I have not done anything to the car to cause this defect.

Please let me know what arrangements you propose for rectifying the problem.

Yours sincerely,

Letter rejecting a dealer's denial of liability

Dear   ,

Re: [make, model and registration number of car]

Thank you for your letter of [date] in which you deny
responsibility for defects in the above car which I
described in my letter of [date].

I have obtained advice which confirms that it is a term
of my contract with you, the seller of the car, that it
should be of merchantable quality. The appearance of
such a major fault so soon in the life of a car indicates
that it was not of merchantable quality when I bought it.
You are, therefore, in breach of contract and I am
entitled to damages. I am prepared to accept [amount],
which is the amount I have been quoted to repair the
fault, or a free repair by your own workshop.

This claim does not affect any rights which I may have
under the manufacturer's warranty.

If I do not receive a satisfactory offer from you within the
next 14 days I intend to ask the Department of
Consumer Affairs to investigate the problem.

Yours sincerely,

Letter to the Department of Consumer Affairs asking them to investigate a complaint

Dear   ,

Re: [make, model and registration number of car]

I am writing to ask you to investigate and help me to resolve a problem which I have regarding the above vehicle.

On [date] I purchased the car from [name and address of dealer]. The car cost [amount] and came with a [period of warranty] warranty. On [date] it developed a major fault [describe fault].

The manager of the authorised service centre to which I took the car told me that the fault must have existed when I bought the car, and that it is not reasonable to expect such a problem so soon in a new car. I obtained a quote for the repair of the car from this service centre and enclose a copy.

I then wrote to the dealer and asked for a free repair. This request was refused because the warranty had expired. I obtained advice about my position from your department and wrote again. I have not received a reply to this letter which was posted 15 days ago. Enclosed are copies of all these letters.

Can you help me please?

Yours sincerely,

Letter rejecting a used car bought from a dealer

Dear   ,

Re: [make, model and registration number of car]

On [date] I bought the above car from you. On [date] I discovered that it had serious defects [describe]. I then took it to a mechanic who examined it and told me that it was unfit to drive.

It was a term of my agreement with you that the vehicle should be of merchantable quality and fit for the purpose for which I bought it. I told your sales assistant that I wanted a reliable car for [describe purpose]. The car is not reliable, and you are, therefore, in breach of contract.

Furthermore, I was persuaded to buy the car by your sales assistant who told me that [describe representations]. This was obviously untrue and the mechanic who examined the car for me told me that he thinks the odometer has been wound back. I think, therefore, that you are liable for misrepresentation as well as breach of contract and that you are guilty of a criminal offence.

I am rejecting the vehicle and expect to be reimbursed for the full purchase price of [amount]. The vehicle can be collected from [address] as soon as I receive your cheque. Failing this, I will be forced to take further action.

Yours sincerely,

Letter to a repairer complaining about workmanship

Dear   ,

Re: [make, model and registration number of car]

On [date] I left the above vehicle at your workshop for [describe repair]. I collected the car on [date] and paid [amount] for the work, which included [specify, if necessary, particular repairs and replacements].

On [date] it developed a serious fault [describe] which cost me [amount] to rectify. A copy of the receipt for that work is enclosed. The mechanic who did the job confirmed that the problem was caused by poor workmanship in the execution of the previous repairs [describe how the work was deficient].

It was an implied term of my contract with you that the work would be carried out with reasonable care and skill. Since you failed to fulfil your part of the bargain, I am entitled to compensation.

I am, therefore, claiming [amount] for expenses incurred as a result of your breach of contract. I look forward to receiving your cheque.

Your sincerely,

Letter disputing excessive charge for service

Dear   ,

Re: [make, model and registration number of car]

On [date], I asked your mechanic to carry out the following repairs on the above vehicle: [describe]. I was told that the work would cost approximately [amount]. When I collected the vehicle, however, I was charged [amount].

I queried the charge but was assured that it was correct. I paid the amount under protest because I needed my car. I was still not happy, however, so I asked two other repairers, [names], to estimate the cost of the work. They quoted [amount] and [amount] respectively, [amount] and [amount] less than your final bill. It is, therefore, clear that your bill was unreasonable.

I am sure that you will agree that there was some mistake in the preparation of my bill. Based on your original estimate and the two other quotes which I obtained, I think that the amount of [amount] would be a reasonable charge. I am, therefore, asking for a refund of [amount].

I look forward to your early reply.

Yours sincerely,

Letter complaining about damage to a vehicle while it was being repaired

Dear   ,

Re: [make, model and registration number of car]

On [date] I left the above vehicle at your workshop for a service. While in your possession it was damaged [describe damage].

You have a duty of care to take reasonable steps to ensure that vehicles in your possession are not damaged. You are also required to exercise reasonable care and skill while carrying out work. The fact that my car was damaged while in your possession indicates that you failed to take reasonable care of it.

I am sure you will agree that I am entitled to ask you to repair the damage at no cost to me. Failing this, I will have the vehicle repaired elsewhere and claim the cost of repairs from you.

Please let me know as soon as possible how you propose to settle this matter. I look forward to your reply.

Yours sincerely,

CHAPTER FIVE

BUILDERS AND OTHER TRADESPEOPLE

The same general law applies to buying services as to buying goods. Every time you engage the services of a builder or painter, gardener or repairer, you enter into a contract with them. As well as the things which you discuss, such as how much the work will cost, there are a range of promises, or warranties, which the law will 'imply' into the contract.

The contract doesn't have to be in writing. To avoid disputes, however, it is always a good idea to ask for, and keep, written evidence, such as quotes, invoices and receipts. If a lot of money is involved, ask for a written contract.

*(**Note:** once you accept a quote, it is binding. The service provider can't charge you more unless the quote specifically provides for extras. If you get an estimate, it is not binding. You can be charged more.)*

What are the implied warranties?

Due Care and Skill

The first promise which the law implies into any contract for services is that the work will be carried out with due care and skill. This means the level of skill and care which an ordinary, competent member of that trade or profession would exercise in the circumstances.

You can't expect an odd-jobs person, for example, to exercise the degree of skill when painting your house that you would expect from a qualified painter. He or she is only expected to meet the standards of ordinary, competent odd-jobs person.

How can you prove that the work was substandard? Sometimes the fact will be self-evident from the damage that has occurred or the faults which exist. Otherwise, get an independent opinion from another service provider (or two) along with a quote for rectifying the problem.

Materials Fit for the Purpose

There is an implied warranty in a contract for services that any materials used will be of reasonable quality and suitable for the purpose for which they are wanted. It doesn't apply, of course, if you told the service provider to use particular materials (although you may then have a claim against the supplier of those materials – see Chapter 3).

The law requires that materials be of 'reasonable' quality. However you may find it difficult to argue that better quality materials should have been used; particularly if you placed a limit on the amount which you were prepared to spend, or if the work was to repair something that was already very old and not expected to last, so that it would have been a waste of money to use new parts or expensive materials.

Services Fit for the Purpose

If you told the service provider that you wanted the work done for a particular purpose, it must be suitable for that purpose.

What Can You Claim?

In most cases it is reasonable to demand a reduction in the agreed price for less than satisfactory services (the reduction may equal the cost of fixing up the problem or the difference between the value of what you asked for and what you got). Alternatively, you may ask the service provider to rectify the problem if that is appropriate.

If the work has to be completely redone, you can claim the cost of undoing what is already there, if necessary, as well as the cost of having it done again.

If the unsatisfactory work caused additional damage – say, for example, a new roof leaked, damaging ceilings, floor coverings and furniture – you may be entitled to claim further compensation for that also.

Remember, you must always do whatever you can to minimise loss or damage. If the roof is leaking, for example, you might be able to provide a temporary cover, put out buckets, move furniture and roll up any rugs. Contact the service provider as soon as you notice the problem. If you delay and thereby make the problem worse, you might not be able to claim for the later damage.

Delays

One of the most common complaints against service providers is the time it takes to get the work done. You are entitled to expect the work to be done in a reasonable time, taking into account all the circumstances, such as weather, conditions in the trade and how long other service providers take to do similar work.

If the contract specifies a time that the work will be done by, you can take action as soon as the period has expired if it also says that 'time is of the essence'. If it doesn't say this, you must write to the service provider giving them a reasonable extra time and stating that you are now making 'time of the essence'.

If a worker doesn't come at the appointed time, you may be able to claim compensation for any financial loss this causes, such as lost wages. This only applies, however, if you told them you would have to take time off work to meet them and they specifically promised to be there at that time. Most service providers refuse to give such undertakings.

Other Problems

What if the expensive evening gown you leave at the dry cleaners' is stolen from their shop?

Service providers have a duty to take reasonable care of any goods left in their possession. If you can prove that they did not take reasonable care – say, for example, the dry cleaner left the shop unattended and unlocked – you can claim compensation.

This may apply, even if a docket or a sign says something like, 'All care but no responsibility'. For such a statement to be part of your contract, the service provider must have taken steps to draw your attention to it before you entered into the contract. Even then, many statutes which give consumers rights specifically state that the service provider cannot 'contract out' of their obligations.

In practice, most service providers are insured and you can claim anyway.

You can also claim compensation if you are injured because of a service provider's carelessness. This is so even if you did not hire them yourself.

Building Work

Building is one area where you should have a written contract. There is usually a lot of money involved and there are countless ways for things to go wrong. Builders must, however, be licensed or registered in most states which means that there is a licensing body to whom you can complain. Compulsory insurance also provides some protection.

Check carefully that your contract covers all aspects of your job – the work that is to be done, materials, time for completion and cost. If your builder doesn't have one prepared, you can get a standard form from the Master Builders' Association.

Make sure you know what is included in the cost and, more importantly, what is not included. The contract might also include some 'provisional' costs for things that the builder can't be sure about the price of until the time comes.

The contract will usually require you to pay in stages. You don't have to agree on a deposit – most materials are supplied on credit – and you should ensure that the contract has a withholding clause. This allows you to delay making the final payment for a time to give the builder an incentive to remedy defects.

The contract should include a clause stating that you are covered if defects appear within a certain time.

Make sure that any changes you decide on are written into the contract.

Taking Action

If your service provider is licensed and, therefore, a member, you might get some help from the relevant trade association. Some trade associations will inspect the work and assist with negotiating a settlement. The Australian Bankers' Association has established an Ombudsman scheme to help with certain disputes. (You can get more information about this facility from pamphlets available at most banks.) If the trader you deal with is licensed, the licensing authority will tell you if there is a dispute resolution body.

If you are not able to resolve your problem by negotiating with the service provider, either with or without the help of a trade association, licensing authority or consumer affairs department, you will have to consider more formal action. This is usually a choice between the Consumer Claims Tribunal (which may be called a commercial or small claims tribunal) in your state or territory, or court action.

Your consumer affairs department, or the relevant trade association, can usually advise you as to the most appropriate course of action.

In general, the tribunals are less expensive (although it now costs $40 to apply to the New South Wales Consumer Claims Tribunal, less for pensioners) and less formal. You do not need to be legally represented and the case is heard by a referee who can order that money be paid or work done. The amount that can be claimed from such tribunals is, however, limited.

Court action for breach of contract may be necessary if the amount of money at stake is too much for a tribunal. In the case of simple matters in the magistrates' courts, the Chamber Magistrate or Clerk of Court may be able to help you to fill in the necessary forms. If the matter is complicated or a large amount of money is involved, you should get legal advice.

If you want disciplinary action taken against the service provider, such as having his or her licence revoked, you should direct your complaint to the relevant licensing authority.

Letter complaining to a builder about unacceptable workmanship

Dear ,

Re: [address of property]

On [date] you finished work on our home. Since then, we have discovered a number of defects, mostly relating to the standard of workmanship: [describe].

Our contract states that you will remedy defects which appear within 6 months of the date of completion. That period is nearly up and I do not intend to make the final payment until all of the above have been rectified.

Please contact me with your proposals for putting the above matters right.

Yours sincerely,

**Letter to licensing body about a dispute with
a builder**

Dear ,

Re: [name and licence number of builder]

I am in dispute with [builder] regarding the
unsatisfactory standard of workmanship at [address]. I
enclose copies of our contract and correspondence
relating to the dispute.

As you will see, I have been unable to reach a
settlement with [builder] and am asking you to assist. I
understand that you have a procedure for investigating
complaints and requiring the builder to rectify defects in
workmanship and materials.

I would be most grateful if you would intervene in this
matter and I look forward to hearing from you.

Yours sincerely,

Letter informing builder that you are appointing another builder to rectify defects

Dear   ,

Re: [address of property]

You have failed to carry out the repairs to my property as requested in my letter of [date], and I have therefore obtained quotes from three other builders, namely [names of builders]; copies of these are enclosed.

As you will see, the quotes show that your work is defective and needs extensive repair. These repairs will cost at least [amount] which is the amount stated in the lowest quote.

I am entitled to expect you to pay for this work, and I therefore look forward to your proposals for settlement. If I do not hear from you within 7 days of the date of this letter I shall go ahead and have the work done by someone else, but you will be required to reimburse me for the repairs undertaken.

Yours sincerely,

Letter claiming the cost of repairs from a builder

Dear   ,

Re: [address of property]

I have received no reply to my letter dated [date]. I have, therefore, engaged [name of builder] to carry out the repairs needed because of your poor workmanship. The work is now complete and cost [amount]. A copy of the invoice is enclosed.

Also enclosed is a copy of a report prepared by [name of builder or whoever prepared the report] which details what was wrong with the work done by you. It shows that you did not use due care and skill. You are, therefore, in breach of contract and I am entitled to expect you to reimburse me for the cost of repairs.

I look forward to receiving your cheque for [amount] within the next 14 days. If you fail to reimburse me I shall have no alternative but to commence legal action without further reference to you,

Yours sincerely,

Letter rejecting a landscaper's bill for more than the original quote

Dear   ,

Re: [quotation number]

I was surprised to see from your invoice [number] of [date] that you have charged me [amount] for [describe work and materials]. Since your original quotation stated that the cost would be [amount], I assume that your invoice was a mistake.

I am aware that the prices quoted for plants and stone were estimates only and I agree that I must pay what these cost you. The amount quoted for the work, however, was a fixed price and it was on the basis of this that I entered into a contract with you.

Though you claim that the increase is due to [describe reasons], this has no bearing on our contract. We did not agree that I would bear the cost of such eventualities. I am only liable for the amount shown in your quotation.

I therefore enclose a cheque for [amount], being the amount originally quoted for carrying out the work plus the actual cost of materials, in full and final settlement of your account.

Yours sincerely,

Letter complaining to an electrician about delays

Dear   ,

Re: [address and quotation number]

I am concerned about your delay in completing the [describe work] contracted for the above property.

Before I accepted your quote you assured me that the work would be completed by [date]. [Period of time] later, it is still not finished. [Detail what remains to be done].

I am afraid that I cannot wait any longer. I am, therefore, making time of the essence. Please finish the work within 14 days from the date of this letter or I shall have to consider our contract at an end. I shall have the work done by another electrician and will deduct the cost from the amount owing to you.

Yours sincerely,

Letter responding to an electrician's failure to complete work

Dear   ,

Re: [address and quotation number]

In my letter dated [date], I asked you to complete the work you have been doing at the above address within 14 days. I am disappointed that you have neither replied to my letter nor completed the work.

I am, therefore, left with no alternative but to consider our contract at an end.

I shall have the work completed by another contractor at your expense. I am obtaining quotes from other electricians and will send you copies in due course.

Yours sincerely,

Letter to a hairdresser about unsatisfactory service causing additional damage

Dear   ,

Re: [unsatisfactory perm and colouring]

On [date] I attended your salon to have [describe the nature of the services requested].

I was most unhappy with the work done by you [outline problems].

You attempted to rectify the problems on [date], but this was not successful [explain why].

I then went to another hairdresser, [name], who explained to me what had gone wrong. I asked him/her to put this in writing and enclose a copy for your information. This report indicates that you did not use due care and skill and were, therefore, in breach of your contract with me.

I not only had to have the work re-done but I also had to have [explain extra service] to repair the damage which you did to my hair. The total cost was [amount]. A copy of my receipt is enclosed.

This incident has cost me a lot of time as well as money and I have been very embarrassed by it. I expect that you will reimburse me for this amount and look forward to receiving your cheque.

Yours sincerely,

Letter to Department of Consumer Affairs regarding hairdresser

Dear   ,

Re: [name of hairdresser]

I am writing to ask your advice and assistance in negotiating a settlement to a dispute which I have with the above hairdresser.

I attempted to resolve the problem myself and even gave him a chance to rectify the damage. When this failed, I consulted another hairdresser who explained the problem and fixed it.

By letter dated [date] I asked [name] to reimburse me for the cost of rectifying the problem. I have had no reply. I have enclosed a copy of this letter which explains in more detail the nature of my complaint. I have also enclosed a copy of a report that I asked the second hairdresser to prepare.

Since I have suffered considerable expense, inconvenience and embarrassment as a result of this hairdresser's failure to exercise due care and skill, I believe that I am entitled to compensation. I would be most grateful if you could tell me where I should go from here.

I look forward to your reply.

Yours sincerely,

Letter asking the Banking Ombudsman to intervene in a dispute

Dear Sir/Madam,

Re: [bank, branch and account number]

I am involved in a dispute with the above bank, which I have been unable to settle by negotiating directly with them. I hope that you will be able to assist.

Briefly, the facts of the matter are these: [briefly, but fully, outline the nature of the dispute, including dates].

Enclosed are copies of [any relevant documents].

You have my authority to obtain any further information from the bank which you think might be relevant.

I look forward to your reply.

Yours sincerely,

Letter to a photographic processor claiming compensation for damaged photographs

Dear   ,

On [date] I left a [describe film] with you for processing. It was damaged [describe how] while in your possession.

The ruined photos were taken [describe the event] and are, therefore, irreplaceable.

The fact that they were damaged while in your possession shows that you failed to use the degree of care and skill that was required under my contract with you. I am, therefore, entitled to compensation, not only for the value of the film but for the loss of enjoyment which I would have derived from the record of this special event.

I think that [amount] would be a reasonable sum of compensation and I look forward to receiving your cheque.

Yours sincerely,

Letter to a washing machine repairer about his failure to keep an appointment

Dear   ,

On [date] I asked you to visit my home to repair my washing machine. At the time I explained to you that it was very difficult for me to be home during business hours, and that I only wanted you to do the job if you could give me a particular date and time when you would be here. You undertook to call on [date and time].

I waited for you for more than 4 hours but you did not come.

Your failure to arrive at the agreed time amounts to a   . breach of your contract with me. I am, therefore, entitled to compensation for both my out-of-pocket expenses [describe] and the inconvenience of having to make alternative arrangements to have my washing machine repaired [describe].

I think that [amount] is a reasonable amount in the circumstances and look forward to receiving your cheque within 14 days.

Yours sincerely,

CHAPTER SIX

PROFESSIONALS

Professionals, such as doctors and lawyers, are service providers. As such, the same general law applies to them as was described in the previous chapter. Consumers who suffer harm as a result of their failure to exercise reasonable care and skill, or because of breaches of contractual duties such as confidentiality, are entitled to sue for compensation.

Not every complaint about a professional person can be resolved in this way, however. Nor should consumers who suffer because of improper or unethical conduct necessarily be put to the trouble and expense of court action. Some complaints can be dealt with by state and territorial consumer affairs departments and tribunals, but there are monetary limits on what these bodies can achieve.

There are also, however, special boards or other bodies which are responsible for regulating professional behaviour. Since professionals must be registered or certified before they can practice, these bodies can apply the ultimate punishment of taking away the person's right to work in his or her profession. If in doubt, your consumer affairs department should be able to tell you which board or organisation will handle your complaint.

In the case of lawyers, doctors and sometimes other health professionals, the role of the professional regulatory bodies has been supplemented, in most states and territories, with independent complaints procedures which are aimed at overcoming the perception that professional people protect each other.

It can be difficult for a client to know whether or not a professional has done a proper job. Most complaints are the result of poor communication. For this reason, it is very important that you insist on explanations, in language which you can understand, of what has been done, what is proposed, why, and how much it will cost. If you are not happy, discuss the matter firstly with the professional involved. If you are still not satisfied, you can take further action.

Lawyers

'Lawyer' is a generic term covering both solicitors and barristers, as well as lawyers working in other fields such as government departments, corporations and universities.

Very generally, solicitors may be described as office lawyers who give advice, draw up documents such as contracts and wills, and assist with negotiating agreements. Barristers are courtroom specialists.

In New South Wales, the profession is presently divided into barristers and solicitors. In other states and territories, lawyers may practise as either barristers or solicitors, or both. The distinction is important because it can affect how you make your complaint.

Most complaints about solicitors should be directed to the Law Society (Law Institute in Victoria) which is the solicitors' professional body. Consumers in South Australia can write to the Legal Practitioners' Complaints Committee. The Law Societies issue solicitors with practising certificates which allow them to practise.

Complaints about barristers may be directed to the Bar Association (Bar Council in Victoria, Barristers' Board in Western Australia, Law Society in Tasmania).

The manner in which complaints are dealt with can, however, vary according to the type of complaint and the state or territory in which you live. It may be a good idea to ring the Society or Association before you write to see whether or not there is a particular committee, council or person to whom you should direct your complaint.

If you are not satisfied with the action taken by the Law Society or Bar Association, there may be another body to which you can appeal. In New South Wales, for example, there are a number of special appeals bodies which deal with different types of matters and which include non-lawyer members. You should be given information about these if your complaint is dismissed. If you are not provided with such information, ask for it. In Victoria, there is the Lay Observer, who performs a similar role.

Consumer affairs departments can also deal with some complaints about lawyers (but not barristers).

All complaints about lawyers should state clearly who you are, who you are complaining about, and what it is that you are complaining about. You should also state what it is that you want – your fees reduced or waived; work done; documents handed over; compensation; or whatever.

If you have lost money because of a solicitor's dishonest handling of his or her trust accounts, you may be able to make a claim on the Fidelity Fund which the Law Societies maintain. In other situations, where you have suffered harm because of a solicitor's negligence, you may be advised to sue for compensation in court.

You cannot sue a barrister for negligence in the manner in which a court case is conducted, but you can sue for negligent advice.

A particular area of concern among consumers of legal services is the question of costs. It is a good idea to discuss this matter and get at least an estimate of the eventual cost before you engage the services of your solicitor or barrister. For some types of legal work there are fixed fees or 'scale' fees which depend on the value of the item involved. Conveyancing fees, for example, depend on the value of the property. 'Disbursements' may be charged on top of the lawyer's fees, however. Disbursements are things which are paid for on your behalf by your solicitor, They might include the cost of photocopying, court filing fees or search fees. Ask about such items at your first visit.

Lawyers can, usually, charge more than the recommended fee if extra time, skill or responsibility is involved. The behaviour of the other party in a dispute may, for example, create a lot of extra work. This makes it difficult for lawyers to give anything more than an initial estimate.

You are entitled to ask for a bill which is sufficiently detailed to let you see how the charges are made up. If you are unsatisfied and your solicitor is not prepared to negotiate, the Law Society may be able to assist. It is possible to have an account 'taxed' (checked) by the court but you risk having to pay a substantial fee if the court does not agree that the solicitor has significantly overcharged you.

Doctors and other Health Professionals

Complaints about lawyers generally have to do with costs, delays, negligence and dishonest handling of money; complaints about doctors and other health professionals most commonly concern negligence, consent to treatment, right to information and confidentiality.

If you have a problem which you cannot resolve directly with the professional concerned, or his or her employer, you need to consider what it is that you wish to achieve.

If you want compensation, you may need to take (or at least threaten) court action. This can be expensive and time-consuming, however, and you have to be able to prove that the professional concerned was negligent or failed to get your consent to the treatment.

Negligence is not taking reasonable care to avoid foreseeable risks. To prove negligence, you need to prove that the person treating you did not live up to the standards of care that ordinary, sensible professionals in the same circumstances would apply. If the case goes to court, you will need to be able to produce some ordinary, sensible professionals to testify on your behalf.

To give a valid consent to treatment, you have to know the nature and effect of what it is that you are consenting to, and any significant risks involved. The treating professional has a responsibility to give you the information that you need to make a sensible decision and, if you have particular concerns, to answer your questions fully. Consent must be freely given. Treatment without a valid consent is an assault, except in cases of emergency.

If you have suffered harm and you believe that it was caused by negligence, assault or, perhaps, breach of contract, you should certainly demand compensation. If your claim is not clear-cut, however, and the professional (or perhaps his or her insurer) disputes it, you will need legal advice about whether or not it is worth going on with the case.

If you want some other kind of action – an apology, to bring poor standards of care to the notice of the authorities, to have the professional disciplined, or whatever – then you should complain to the relevant professional registration board. Address your complaint to the 'Registrar'.

There are also special health complaints bodies. Usually called Complaints Units within the state Health Departments (in New South Wales the Health Care Complaints Commission; in South Australia the Health Advice and Complaints Office; and in Victoria the Office of the Health Services Commissioner), these bodies will give advice, investigate complaints and attempt to negotiate a solution. In suitable cases, they may refer the matter to a professional board or other relevant body. They do not represent individuals, however, in compensation cases.

Letter asking a solicitor for an itemised account

Dear   ,

Re: Client [your name], Invoice No. [number]

Thank you for your letter of [date] containing your account for [amount].

So that I can get a clearer understanding of the component parts of your bill, I would be grateful if you would provide me with a breakdown of the items involved. In particular, how do your charges compare with the Law Society's recommended fees for similar work?

I understand that I will not be charged extra for the work involved in preparing an itemised bill.

I look forward to your reply.

Yours sincerely,

Letter disputing the amount charged by a solicitor

Dear   ,

Re: [invoice number]

Thank you for your letter of [date] containing a detailed breakdown of your account.

I do have some concern about the amount you have charged. [State where you think overcharging has occurred and why you think the amount is unfair.]

In the circumstances, I think that [amount] is a more reasonable fee for the services you have rendered and enclose my cheque for this amount.

Should you disagree with me on this matter, I suggest we ask the Law Society to adjudicate. Please let me have your views as soon as possible.

Yours sincerely,

Letter to a solicitor complaining about delays

Dear   ,

Re: [nature of work, for example, Sale of 12 Three St, Fourville]

I instructed you to undertake [type of work] on my behalf on [date]. I am, however, concerned about the amount of time it is taking.

Please would you let me know what has been done, why it has taken so long to get to the present stage, what remains to be done and how long you expect this to take.

I would also like to know what costs I have incurred so far and what you estimate the total cost will be.

I look forward to your prompt reply.

Yours sincerely,

Letter to the Law Society complaining about a solicitor

Dear   ,

Re: [name of solicitor]

I would like to complain about the above solicitor whom I instructed on [date] to perform [nature of work] on my behalf.

I am dissatisfied with the manner in which he/she has acted for me for the following reasons: [detail problem].

In the circumstances, I think that I am entitled to [an apology, refund, compensation, have work done, etc.]

I have enclosed copies of all relevant correspondence and my own statement of the events leading up to this problem. If you need any more information, please contact me.

I would be most grateful for your assistance in resolving this problem and look forward to hearing from you in due course.

Yours sincerely,

Letter to a doctor claiming compensation

Dear   ,

Re: [nature of treatment]

On [date] I consulted you because of [briefly describe symptoms] and you [describe nature of treatment].

As a result of this treatment, I suffered a number of problems. [Describe].

After consulting another doctor, I believe that you failed to exercise reasonable care and skill in relation to my health care. [Detail the reasons why you believe this].

I am, therefore, asking you to compensate me for [detail amount claimed for lost wages, medical and other expenses, pain and suffering, long term injury and disability as appropriate. If the harm is substantial, consult a solicitor] .

Please let me have your reply within 14 days.
Yours sincerely,

Letter to a medical complaints unit about a doctor's conduct

Dear   ,

Re: [doctor's name and practice]

I wish to complain about the quality of service I received from the above doctor.

On [date], I consulted Dr [name] because [describe].

Despite the fact that I had an appointment I was forced to wait for [time]. When I finally saw the doctor his/her behaviour was unsatisfactory because [describe].

I was not happy with the diagnosis so I sought a second opinion from Dr [name of second doctor]. He/she diagnosed [describe] and I was treated for this condition. I am now much improved.

The behaviour of Dr [name] was unacceptable and I believe that he/she should be disciplined. I would, therefore, be grateful if you would investigate his/her conduct.

I look forward to hearing from you in due course.

Yours sincerely,

Letter to Psychologists' Registration Board about a psychologist's behaviour

Dear   ,

Re: [psychologist's name and address of practice]

I wish to complain about the behaviour of the above psychologist.

When I attended his/her rooms on [date], his/her behaviour was unprofessional [describe]. Because of what happened, I was unable to go through with the appointment and left.

I would be grateful if you would investigate my complaint and take appropriate action.

I look forward to your reply in due course.

Yours sincerely,

CHAPTER SEVEN
NEIGHBOURS

Our homes are our private domains where we can relax and be ourselves away from the pressures of the outside world. Under the law, we are entitled to 'quiet enjoyment' of the property we occupy. Anything which unreasonably interferes with this is a 'nuisance' and we can get a court order to stop it.

Unfortunately, not all neighbours agree on what is 'reasonable'. Crying babies, leafy trees, swimming pool pumps, pets, music practice, old cars, mischievous children and house extensions can all interfere with quiet enjoyment. But are these interferences unreasonable? Obviously, living in towns and cities, some disturbances are inevitable. Tolerance and understanding are necessary if you want to live peacefully alongside your neighbours.

On the other hand, neighbours do sometimes overstep the mark. This doesn't mean that they are selfish pigs or uncivilised barbarians. They may not have realised that they are disturbing you, or they may have been feeling a bit guilty about it. A friendly conversation may be all that is needed to stop the problem or to work out a compromise that suits you both.

Taking Suitable Action

An officious letter threatening legal action is likely to turn a perfectly nice neighbour into a raving maniac who will spend the next twenty years trying to make your life a misery.

'Putting it in writing' should be a last resort where neighbours are concerned. You may need to write because you and your neighbours are rarely home at the same time, because verbal attempts to solve the problem have failed or because you want to create a written record of an agreement which you have reached. Keep the tone of such letters friendly and polite – no matter how you are feeling.

Take extra care if your neighbour's first language is different from your own. A person who can communicate reasonably well verbally, assisted by facial expressions and body language, can easily misunderstand a written message. Try to understand cultural differences and make allowances for them.

Consider mediation before you take more drastic legal action. Mediators are trained to help people reach their own settlements. Unlike courts, they do not make judgements about who is right and who is wrong. A mediated settlement of a neighbourhood dispute is more likely to bring about a long-term solution to your problems than bringing in the police or issuing a summons. There are Community Justice Centres or Neighbourhood Mediation Centres in most states and territories.

Fences

Good fences might make good neighbours but the process of building and repairing them can ruin neighbourly relations forever. Disputes can arise over the type of fence, its position and whether or not one is needed in the first place. One neighbour might also object if he or she believes that the other, or his or her children, have caused the damage which has led to the need for repairs or replacements.

The rules about dividing fences vary slightly from state to state. In general, however, adjoining neighbours must share the cost of building and repairing dividing fences.

If you cannot come to a friendly agreement about the fence, you can compel your neighbour to share the cost by giving him or her written notice that you want to carry out the work. The letter should say where the fence will go and the type of fence you plan to build. It should be accompanied by one or more quotes for a fence of the type normally found in your neighbourhood (you would have to pay for the extra cost of anything fancy). Give your neighbour a month to consider the plan and perhaps obtain extra quotes. If he or she does not then agree, either of you can seek an order from your local magistrate's court.

You can then go ahead and construct the fence and, if your neighbour does not contribute, you can go back to the court to enforce the order.

The procedure for repairs is similar. Give your neighbour a letter asking him or her to share the cost. If he or she does not agree, you can carry out the repairs and get a court order requiring him or her to pay.

Even if you and your neighbour are in full agreement, it is a good idea to send a letter confirming the details and enclosing quotes.

Noise

Unreasonable noise can amount to a 'nuisance' and you are entitled to a court order to stop it. It might also contravene laws in your state or territory which set specific rules about noise levels and the times within which noisy activities must be confined. These laws divide responsibility for enforcement between police, local councils and state and territorial environmental protection authorities.

Some noise from adjoining properties is inevitable. Ordinary noise is not unreasonable unless it occurs with unreasonable frequency, at unreasonable hours or at unreasonable levels. If you are concerned, and a friendly chat with your neighbour does not result in improvement, you might write to them, explaining why you find the noise so difficult to live with and offering some solutions.

If this doesn't work, find out more about your options from your local court, council, the police, or state environmental protection body.

Trees

Trees are a source of disputation because they block out sunlight, drop leaves and branches, damage pipes and paving, and occasionally fall over.

If a tree damages your property, you might be entitled to some compensation (see Compensation for Damage, below). If you want to cut back overhanging branches or encroaching roots at your boundary, you are entitled to do so, provided that you are not breaching any local tree preservation order. You should also ask the neighbours if they would like the cut branches returned to their property.

Trespassers

A person who enters land without permission, or refuses to leave when asked to, is a trespasser. You can forcibly remove a trespasser, provided that you do not use more force than is reasonably necessary. It is wiser to call the police than to risk being charged with assault. You can also sue a trespasser for compensation for any damage done.

If you set traps for trespassers, or do anything else which harms them, they can sue you. If children come onto your property from time to time, take particular care to ensure that there is nothing there that might injure them.

The unauthorised entry of an object (including an animal) onto your land can also be a trespass. If the object causes damage, you are entitled to keep it until compensation for the damage is paid.

Compensation for Damage

If something escapes from your neighbour's property onto your own, and does damage, you are entitled to compensation. The entry might amount to a trespass (as when a ball is thrown or a hose is directed), a nuisance (smoke and ashes from a fire, water from pipes), or negligence (as when an old tree falls or pesticide spray drifts onto your property).

The only exception is when the damage is caused by a natural event or situation, such as a flood, or a storm or the slope of the land, and not by any intentional or careless act or omission by your neighbour.

You can also sue for negligence if your neighbour's failure to take reasonable care to avoid a foreseeable risk results in damage to you or your property, even though nothing actually crosses the boundary. An example might be excavation work which undermines your foundations.

Letter giving notice of intention to build a dividing fence

Dear   ,

I would like to arrange to have a fence built on the boundary between our two properties, and I understand that we will each be responsible for one-half of the cost.

I have obtained a quote for an ordinary paling fence and enclose a copy for your consideration. Also enclosed is a diagram showing exactly where the fence will go. Please let me know as soon as possible if this is satisfactory.

I am at home most evenings if you would like to discuss the matter further. You are welcome to call in or to telephone me on [number].

Yours sincerely,

Letter disputing the type of fence proposed

Dear   ,

I agree that we should erect a fence between our properties. I cannot, however, afford a sandstone wall.

My budget does not run to more than an ordinary paling fence. Enclosed is a quote. You will see that half the cost is [amount] and I am willing to contribute that amount.

I am sorry that I cannot offer more. I agree that sandstone would look very nice.

Yours sincerely,

Letter to a neighbour who refuses to share the cost of repairs

Dear   ,

I would like to repair the hole in the fence between our two properties. [Explain any particular reasons which you have for wanting the fence repaired].

I know that you do not agree with me about this, but I have been advised that I am entitled to go ahead and have the work done. If you do not contribute your half share of the cost, I can obtain a court order requiring you to pay.

Enclosed is a quote for your consideration. If I do not hear from you within a month I will tell the contractor to start work.

I am sorry that this issue has disturbed an otherwise amicable relationship. Please contact me if you would like to talk about it some more. Perhaps we can reach a compromise.

Yours sincerely,

Letter complaining about noise

Dear   ,

I am writing to ask you to reduce [describe the
offending noise].

You may not have realised how much it affects us but
we cannot put up with it any longer. [Describe any
particular problems or discomforts caused by the noise].

I am sorry to write to you like this and I hope that you
will not be offended. I would, however, be most
grateful for your cooperation in this matter.

Yours sincerely,

Letter complaining to local council about noise

Dear   ,

Re: noise from [address]

I am writing to complain about noise emanating from the above address. [Describe noise, its level and frequency].

I have spoken to my neighbour about the problem and have written to him without success. A copy of my letter to him is enclosed. While I accept that some noise is inevitable, I do not think the level and frequency in this case is reasonable. Other local residents agree. [Describe particular problems or discomforts caused by the noise].

I understand that Council has some powers to control noise of this type. I would be most grateful if you would take action in this case and am available at the above address if you require any further information.

Yours sincerely,

Letter to neighbour about an overhanging tree

Dear   ,

I am writing to let you know that the branches of your [type] tree which overhang my property are causing me some problems [describe].

I have checked with council that there is no tree preservation order affecting the tree and have their permission to lop the offending branches. I intend, therefore, to carry out the work this weekend.

I know you like the tree so I will try not to spoil its overall appearance. I understand that I should put the lopped branches back on your property. Would you prefer me to dispose of them myself?

Please call me if you wish to discuss this matter further.

Yours sincerely,

Letter complaining about damage caused by tree roots

Dear   ,

As you know, I have noticed [describe damage and period of time in which it has been developing], caused by the roots of your [describe] tree.

Since we have not been able to agree on a solution in our talks about this matter, I have obtained an expert opinion that it is the roots which have done the damage and also a quote for its repair. Copies are enclosed.

It is important that the problem is fixed now before it gets any worse.

Since you are responsible for the damage, I need to know how you wish to proceed. Do you want to do the repairs yourself or should I have the work done and send you an account? You are welcome to inspect the damage.

Please let me have your decision within 14 days.

I am sorry to have to write to you in this manner and hope it will not spoil our friendly association.

Yours sincerely,

Letter complaining about trespass

Dear   ,

As we have discussed on a number of occasions, I do not want [name of person/s] coming onto my property without my permission. [Describe any particular reasons why not, such as security, their safety, the fact that they are doing damage, or your desire for privacy].

I find, however, that the trespass continues and I am being forced to consider court action to stop it. While I am not happy about taking such a step, I can see no alternative.

Please stop [name of person] coming onto my property without my permission. If it happens again, I shall commence legal action without further notice.

Yours sincerely,

CHAPTER EIGHT

GOVERNMENT AGENCIES

It is traditional in Australia to 'knock' public servants. Many of them are undoubtedly hard-working, dedicated professionals. However, they are paid with our money, and their actions (or inactions) can have dramatic, often catastrophic, effects on our lives and we are, therefore, entitled to insist on fairness, competence and honesty.

If you are dissatisfied with a decision made or an action taken by a government agency (or with the fact that they haven't done something), you should complain first to the officer concerned. If this doesn't achieve the result you want, ask to have the matter reviewed by someone higher in the organisation. Only when this fails should you take more formal action.

State or Federal?

Australia has a federal system of government. We have a Commonwealth (or Federal) Government which is responsible for matters affecting the whole country, such as taxation, social security, immigration, defence and interstate and international trade and commerce. We also have state and territorial governments. They have their own areas of responsibility, including education, health, housing, police and community welfare.

Local government is often seen as the third level of government but it is ultimately controlled by the state governments.

It is important to be clear about which level of government you are dealing with because you don't want to waste time complaining to the wrong people.

Ombudsmen

The Ombudsman investigates complaints about government bodies and tries to remedy them. There is a Commonwealth Ombudsman (with branches in each state and territory) and one in every state. It doesn't cost anything to complain.

Letters of complaint should include:
- Copies of any correspondence with the agency or department;
- The facts of the dispute;
- The reason for your complaint; and
- What you would like to have done about it.

The Ombudsmen cannot investigate complaints about government ministers, judges, magistrates or coroners. They cannot get involved in employment disputes between government agencies and their employees, and some government departments are excluded. When they do investigate, they have the power to go into offices, to investigate files and other documents, and to speak with the people concerned.

The Ombudsmen resolve most problems informally. If they think that a government agency has acted wrongly, however, they will issue a report, making recommendations. They cannot order the government agency concerned to do anything, but if the agency does not accept their recommendations, they can report the matter to parliament and thus bring it to the attention of the media.

Special Courts and Tribunals

Sometimes you are entitled to appeal against the decision

of a government official to a special court or tribunal. If you are adversely affected by a decision you should always ask about your right to appeal.

The Administrative Appeals Tribunal hears appeals against a wide range of decisions made by Commonwealth Government agencies. To find out if it can help you, contact the registry in your capital city. Another federal body is the Social Security Appeals Tribunal which hears appeals against decisions concerning pensions and benefits. Some states and territories have Welfare Rights Centres which specialise in giving legal advice about Social Security matters.

In all cases, it is important to act quickly. There may be time limits when you can apply.

Freedom of Information

If you have a problem with a government agency, it is important that you get as much information as possible about how and why the agency acted (or failed to act) before you make your complaint. You can often get this information by asking for access to particular documents under Freedom of Information laws.

There is a federal Freedom of Information Act and separate laws in the states and territories. The detailed rules concerning the information you are entitled to access, and the cost of obtaining access, vary from place to place.

You should request access to documents in writing, giving the agency concerned enough information to identify the documents you want.

Judicial Review

It is possible to take government agencies to court if they

have acted unfairly, have failed to carry out their legal responsibilities or have exceeded their powers under the law. Get legal advice before considering action of this type.

Letter to the Ombudsman

Dear   ,

Re: [name of department or agency]

I am writing to complain about the conduct of the above department.

[Give a clear statement of what happened, including dates and names of any particular officers concerned]. I enclose copies of my correspondence with the [name of agency] to date.

I consider that the [name of agency] has acted [unfairly/ incompetently/ dishonestly] because [state the substance of your complaint].

I would like them to [state what you would like to achieve by your complaint].

I would be most grateful if you would investigate this matter and I look forward to your reply.

Yours sincerely,

Letter to a government agency seeking information

Dear   ,

I am writing to request copies of the following documents under the Freedom of Information laws: [list documents, giving as much identifying information as possible, including names and dates].

I enclose [amount] which I understand is the fee for this request. Please let me know if this amount is incorrect.

I look forward to your reply,

Yours sincerely,

Letter of complaint to a government agency

Dear [name of head of department or section] ,

I am writing to complain about the manner in which I have been treated by officers of your department/agency.

[Describe what happened clearly and objectively, including names and dates].

I consider that I have been treated unfairly/ incompe-tently/ rudely/ dishonestly because [state the substance of your complaint]. I have spoken with the officer/s concerned about my dissatisfaction but we have not been able to resolve the problem.

I think that I am entitled to expect [state what you hope to achieve by your complaint].

I would be most grateful if you would investigate this matter with a view to remedying the situation.

Yours sincerely,

Letter asking for a review of a decision

Dear   ,
On [date] I was notified that [describe decision].

I do not agree with this decision because [briefly describe reasons].

I am, therefore, asking you to arrange to have the matter reviewed by another officer of your department/agency. I will be happy to supply any further information which he or she may require.

I look forward to your reply.

Yours sincerely,

CHAPTER NINE

INSURANCE

When you buy insurance, you enter into a contract with the insurer – just as you do with any other provider of goods or services. The policy contains the terms of your agreement. Insurance contracts, however, have some special features.

It is a term of every insurance contract that both parties – the consumer and the insurer – will act with the 'utmost good faith'. This means that the insurer will give the consumer ('the insured') all the information which he or she needs to make sensible decisions about whether or not to enter into the contract.

The insured, on the other hand, must not make any false or exaggerated claims and must cooperate with the insurer.

There is also a 'duty of disclosure' with insurance contracts. When you enter into a contract for insurance you must let the insurer know about anything which might affect their decision to insure you. In other words, you must answer all the questions they ask fully and honestly. If you deliberately give false information, the insurer can refuse to pay your claims. If you inadvertently fail to disclose a 'material' fact, or make an honest mistake when filling out the forms, the amount that they pay you may be reduced.

Buying Insurance

There are three types of insurance policies:
- A 'material damage' policy insures specific items against damage from a variety of causes. House contents insurance is an example. It is important to be

clear about whether you are insuring for full replacement value with a new item, for an 'agreed' value, or for an 'indemnity' or market value.

- A 'liability' policy covers you for liability to pay damages in the event that you are negligent. Third party property insurance for motor vehicles is 'liability' insurance.
- 'Promised benefits' policies pay an amount of money if certain events happen – if, for example, you can't work because of sickness, accidents or unemployment. Life insurance policies are 'promised benefits' policies.

It is worthwhile shopping around for insurance. The cheaper policies are usually more limited than the others so you should be quite clear about what you are missing out on. Compare the benefits offered by the different companies.

You can buy insurance directly from the company concerned, through an insurance broker, an insurance agent or through some other intermediary such as a bank. Insurance brokers act as your agent. Insurance agents, on the other hand, are acting for the insurance company.

Most companies will give you a 'cover note' which means that you are covered, free of charge, while negotiations are finalised for a policy. Once the policy is signed, however, it is backdated to the beginning of the time covered by the cover note.

Making a Claim

If you want to make a claim you should, as soon as possible, notify the insurer. They will let you know what forms you have to fill out and any other papers you might need. They will usually appoint an adjustor, or assessor, to work out how much they should pay and that person has to act fairly towards both parties. (In some cases, such as car accidents, you are obliged to notify your insurer even if you don't want to make a claim. Check your policy.)

When you first contact the insurer (usually by telephone) ask about the effect of the claim on any no-claim bonus you might have and whether or not you must make an excess payment. You might need to consider at this point whether or not claiming on your policy is worthwhile.

The company will refuse to pay if they think that your claim is fraudulent. It may, for example, be exaggerated, or deliberately false, or it may be made by someone who is not entitled to claim. If you disagree with their refusal to pay, you can go to court. Even if part of your claim is exaggerated, the court can order the insurer to pay some of the money. On the other hand, it is a crime to make a false claim. The insurer must, in such a case, report the matter to the police. They are also entitled to get any money they have paid out back.

The insurer may also refuse to pay the claim if you have caused the loss which gives rise to the claim. If, for example, you have not had your brakes checked when they should have been checked and an accident results, the insurer may decide to pay you less or nothing at all.

If you are not satisfied by the insurance company's offer, write to them, explaining your reasons. If you are still dissatisfied, approach either the Life Insurance Complaints Board or the Claims Review Panel (for general insurance). Your state or territorial consumer affairs department may also provide you with advice and assistance. Where appropriate, the dispute can be heard before the Consumer Claims Tribunal or its equivalent in your state.

Letter informing an insurer of a claim on building insurance

Dear   ,

Re: [policy number]

As we discussed on the telephone on [date], I wish to make a claim on the above policy.

On [date] my property was damaged by [describe the circumstances]. As it was an emergency, I called in [appropriate professional] who carried out emergency repairs [describe briefly]. This work cost [amount].

I wish to claim for the emergency work as well as for the eventual cost of repairing the damage properly.

Please send me the appropriate claim form.

Yours sincerely,

Letter rejecting company's denial of
liability

Dear   ,

Re: [policy number]

I wish to dispute your rejection of my claim on the
grounds that [state reason why claim was rejected].

The policy states that [quote wording]. The damage to
my property was caused by [cause] and was not due to
[neglect, etc] as you suggest. I have enclosed a report
from [relevant expert] which supports my argument
[details of report].

I believe that I am covered by the terms of this policy
and am entitled to the amount claimed. I would be
grateful if you would review your decision to reject my
claim and let me have your answer as soon as
possible.

Yours sincerely,

Final letter to an insurance company in a dispute over a building claim

Dear   ,

Re: [policy number]

On [date] I claimed on this policy for [describe damage] which occurred on [date].

Although you have reviewed the matter and upheld your original rejection of my claim, I believe that I have supplied sufficient evidence to you in the form of [describe] to prove that my claim is covered by the policy.

I believe that I have been unfairly treated and unless you can offer some proposals for settlement within 14 days, I intend to refer my complaint to the Claims Review Panel and/or take legal action.

Yours sincerely,

Letter rejecting an insurance company's offer

Dear   ,

Re: [policy number]

Thank you for your letter dated [date], offering [amount] for my [item] which was [detail loss/damage] on [date].

I do not agree, however, with your assessment of the item's value. I have enclosed a valuation certificate made by [name of valuer] which states that the [item] was worth [amount].

Please reconsider your offer in the light of this evidence. I look forward to hearing from you,

Yours sincerely,

Letter claiming on holiday insurance

Dear   ,

Re: [policy number]

I wish to make a claim on the above holiday insurance policy.

I have just returned from [location]. I was there between [dates]. On [date] my [item], worth [amount] was [stolen, damaged etc]. I reported the matter to the police on the same day and can confirm this.

Please send me the appropriate claim form.

Yours sincerely,

Letter claiming for a cancelled holiday

Dear   ,

Re: [policy number]

On [date] I booked a holiday [describe dates and location] with [travel agent].

I am now unable to take the holiday because [describe reason]. I have written to the agent cancelling my booking and I have obtained a medical report as evidence of my incapacity.

My holiday insurance covers me for the full cost of the holiday in the event that it has to be cancelled or cut short because of illness or injury. I intend, therefore, to claim on the policy and would be grateful if you would send me the appropriate claim form. Please let me know if there is any other information which you might need to process my claim.

Yours sincerely,

Letter to Claims Review Panel about a dispute with an insurer

Dear   ,

Re: [insurance company and policy number]

I am in dispute with the above insurance company and would like to ask for your assistance in resolving the matter.

I have been unable to reach a settlement with the company in respect of its rejection of my claim. I enclose copies of all the relevant correspondence. As I stated therein, I believe that I have been treated unfairly because [briefly explain reasons].

I would be very grateful if you would investigate this matter and I look forward to hearing from you in due course.

Yours sincerely,

CHAPTER TEN

ACCIDENTS AND INJURIES

If you are harmed by the negligence of others, you are entitled to damages (compensation) for the harm done.

Usually, you would write to the negligent party and, if the matter is clear-cut, the claim is paid by them, or their insurer. If they dispute the claim, however, you may need to consider court action.

To prove that they were negligent you would have to be able to satisfy a court on a number of points:

- That they owed you a duty of care. This means that they knew, or ought to have known, that you could be affected by their acts and omissions. Road users, for example, owe other road users a duty of care. The occupiers of houses and flats, shopping malls and sporting venues all owe a duty of care to the people who come onto those premises. Service providers have a duty of care to their clients.
- That they breached their duty of care. You must be able to satisfy a court that they failed to take reasonable care to avoid foreseeable risks. In deciding what is reasonable, the court would look at what ordinary, sensible people in the same situation would have done.
- That harm has been suffered. You may have suffered personal injury or illness, emotional trauma, financial loss, property damage or less tangible harm such as pain and suffering or loss of enjoyment of life.
- That the harm was caused by the negligence.

Sometimes, more than one person is to blame. You may have contributed to your injury yourself. In this case, the court would apportion blame among those who were negligent.

This is the basic common law of negligence. In some circumstances, parliaments have made laws which modify the common law for particular types of accidents.

Occupier's Liability

The responsibilities of people who occupy premises towards those who come onto them used to be extremely complicated. It depended on how the person came to be there – whether they had paid for the privilege, had been invited, were merely tolerated or were trespassers.

Recent High Court decisions have changed the law so that the ordinary rules of negligence apply. If you want to claim compensation from an occupier you must show that he or she failed to take reasonable care for your safety. Whether you were a trespasser or an invited guest would be relevant to the question of what is 'reasonable'.

In general, occupiers should ensure that premises are reasonably safe for the people who come there – floors should be kept clean and free from obstacles, stairs and other structures should be in good repair – and visitors should be warned about any hidden dangers such as slippery surfaces, holes in the ground, wet paint and so on.

Work Accidents

If you are injured at work through the negligence of your employer you may be able to claim damages at common law. In some states, however, the right to seek common law damages has been abolished or limited to cases involving serious harm.

Most workers who suffer injuries or work-related illnesses are entitled to workers' compensation. This is compensation for lost wages, for expenses and damage to property, and for permanent loss or loss of use of body parts or functions. If a worker is killed, his or her dependants are entitled to compensation. All employers must carry workers' compensation insurance.

Workers' compensation (known as Workcare or Workcover in some states) is cheaper and easier to obtain than common law damages because you don't have to prove that your injury or illness was caused by the fault of anyone else. It is enough that it happened in the course of your employment or arose out of your employment. The only time that you are not entitled to compensation is when your injury is intentionally self-inflicted or caused solely by your serious and wilful misconduct. Even then, compensation will be paid if the injury results in your death or serious and permanent disablement.

The benefits payable under workers' compensation are not usually as high, however, as the damages that can be awarded under the common law.

You must notify your employer of all accidents and injuries as soon as they happen. To claim compensation, you must get a claim form from your employer and complete it. You then give the form, plus a doctor's certificate and any other supporting information, to your employer who sends it to the insurer. The insurer may ask you to undergo a medical examination.

Most claims are paid and you collect your money through your employer. Sometimes, however, the insurer will refuse the claim or will terminate payments. This might happen, for example, if they are not satisfied about the extent of your incapacity. If this happens, you can appeal against it to a special court or board. The procedure varies from state to state.

While you are awaiting the outcome of your appeal, you may be entitled to Sickness Benefits or a Disability Support Pension. If you ultimately receive your workers' compensation for the whole period you will be asked to repay any Social Security money you have received.

Motor Vehicle Accidents

The ordinary laws of negligence apply to accidents which involve motor vehicles but laws relating to compulsory insurance affect the practical steps you should take in the event of an accident. You can get more information about the provisions in your state or territory from your insurer, your motorist's association or from one of the law handbooks which have been produced by Community Legal Centres in each state and territory.

In general, you should get the names and addresses of all witnesses immediately after an accident. Make notes, including details of any conversations which you had with other people at the scene, and diagrams showing what happened. Do not admit any blame on your part or you could invalidate your insurance.

Make sure you have the other driver's name and address, the registration number of the vehicle and the name of the company it is insured with.

Report the accident to your insurer, even if you haven't decided whether or not to make a claim.

Motor vehicle accidents can result in two types of injury: property damage and personal injury. Since different insurance policies usually apply to each of these, you may have to claim compensation separately.

The police might charge a driver after the accident but these criminal proceedings have nothing to do with the civil action necessary to get compensation. Criminal convictions, even for negligent driving, can't be used to prove that the other driver was negligent in the civil sense.

If your vehicle is damaged, you have three options: you can claim on your own policy; pay for the repairs; or demand payment from the other party.

If you have comprehensive insurance, let your insurer handle the claim, unless you prefer not to claim on your policy. The amount of excess payable or the loss of your no-claim bonus may mean that it is not worth your while, financially. On the other hand, some companies allow you to keep your no-claim bonus if the accident was not your fault and they are ultimately able to get damages from the other party.

By claiming on your policy, you can get your car repaired with a minimum of delay.

If you are not covered for damage to your own vehicle, you will have to either pay for the repairs yourself, or claim damages from the other party. If they are uninsured and cannot afford to pay for the damage, there is not much point in suing them. Your costs might outweigh what you ultimately get back. It is always worth writing to them and claiming damages, however. You can decide later whether or not it is worth taking all the way to court. At this point get further information and advice from a solicitor or from one of the sources mentioned above.

Personal injuries are generally covered by compulsory third-party insurance. The procedures for making a claim vary from place to place, and you will need to get further information about what to do in your particular case.

Letter claiming damages for injury

Dear   ,

On [date] I was injured when [describe accident].

As a result of this accident I suffered [detail injuries].

My injuries were caused by your negligence in that you [describe negligence, for example, failed to keep floor clean, or to warn of danger].

I am, therefore, claiming [amount] in damages. This amount is made up as follows [list out of pocket expenses, lost wages, etc – get legal advice if your claim is substantial or you have suffered permanent injuries]. Enclosed is a copy of a medical report [and any other relevant documents] which substantiates my claim.

Please let me know as soon as possible your proposals for settling this claim.

Yours sincerely,

Letter rejecting other party's denial of liability

Dear   ,

On [date] I received your letter denying liability for [describe damage].

I do not accept your reasons for refusing my claim and repeat that I am holding you responsible for the harm I have suffered. [Explain why you believe the other party was negligent].

You say that you have rejected my claim because [state reasons]. I would refute this by pointing out [provide information and arguments].

If I do not receive a satisfactory offer from you within 14 days of the date of this letter, I shall commence legal action.

Yours sincerely,

Letter to employer regarding workers' compensation claim

Dear   ,

On [date] I was injured in an accident at work. As a result of that accident I suffered [describe injuries].

I reported the accident at the time to [name and title of person in authority] and went on sick leave. I would now like to claim workers' compensation because it seems that I will need more time off work.

Would you please send me the relevant forms and information so that I can submit my claim as soon as possible.

Yours sincerely,

Letter in response to refusal of workers' compensation

Dear   ,

Re: [claim number]

I have today received notification of your refusal of my claim for workers' compensation. You state that [reasons for refusal of claim].

I must ask you to reconsider my claim. I believe that I am entitled to workers' compensation because [state why claim should be paid, including medical and other evidence].

Enclosed are additional and more recent medical reports in support of my claim. I am happy to submit to any further examinations you may require and to supply any further information which may be necessary.

I look forward to your reply,

Yours sincerely,

Letter of demand for motor vehicle damage

Dear ,

I am the owner of motor vehicle number [registration number] that was damaged in a collision with your vehicle on [date] at [place].

I believe that the accident was your fault because [describe reasons]. I am, therefore, asking you to pay for the repair of my vehicle. .

The damage has been assessed at [amount] and a copy of the quotation is enclosed. [It is preferable to have obtained more than one quote – this will help you to establish that the amount you are claiming is reasonable.] If you are insured, please forward this letter to your insurers as soon as possible. Otherwise, please let me know whether you regard the assessment as reasonable and intend to pay for the damage.

If you wish to inspect the damage, please call me on [telephone number].

I look forward to hearing from you soon,

Your sincerely,

Letter to insurance company

Dear Sir or Madam,

Re : accident involving your insured [other driver's name]

I am the owner of motor vehicle number [registration number] that was involved in an accident with vehicle number [registration number] at [place] on [date]. That vehicle is owned by [name] and is insured by you.

I enclose a copy of a letter that I have sent to him/her claiming the cost of repairs to my vehicle. Also enclosed is a quotation for the repairs. I am happy to provide any further information which you may require.

I look forward to your reply.

Yours faithfully,

Second letter of demand

Dear   ,

On [date] I wrote to you about the accident on [date] at [place]. I asked you to contact me regarding compensation for the damage to my vehicle which was caused by your negligence.

[Amount of time – give them two weeks] have now passed and I have received no reply from you. I must now inform you, therefore, that unless I receive [amount] within 14 days of today's date, I shall commence legal action to enforce my claim.

Yours sincerely,

CHAPTER ELEVEN
CREDIT AND DEBT

Obtaining finance can be stressful and confusing. There are so many different types of credit available that it is difficult to compare costs and benefits. Consumer credit laws have, however, been passed to ensure that contracts between consumers and credit providers are fair to both parties.

The laws apply only to consumer credit dealings – commercial transactions and large borrowings are regulated by ordinary contract law. They also vary slightly from state to state. Get advice from a consumer credit legal service, financial counsellor, consumer affairs department or a solicitor if you are in trouble. If necessary, disputes can be resolved by a special credit tribunal.

If you can't pay, it is imperative that you contact the credit provider and attempt to negotiate a solution. Generally, they will only take legal action against you if there is no alternative. Ignoring the problem will result in further costs for you to pay.

Your Rights

Borrowers under consumer contracts have some basic rights.

Most importantly, the contract should not be unjust. If unfair tactics were used to induce the consumer to enter into the contract, the interest is excessive or its terms are harsh or oppressive, you can ask the credit tribunal (or commercial tribunal) to look at it. The tribunal will, if it agrees that the contract is unjust, take appropriate steps to remedy the situation.

Consumers have a right to information. The contract must be easy to read and understand, you must be given a copy before you sign it, and it must clearly set out the full cost of the arrangement. The contract itself must warn you not to sign unless you understand it. And the credit provider must send you more information about your rights and responsibilities after you sign. It is still up to you to actually read the information, however, and to make sure that you understand it.

To make it easier for you to compare costs between different credit providers, they must be calculated according to a set formula and expressed as an 'annual percentage rate'.

Borrowers also have the right not to have goods repossessed unless proper procedures are followed. You must be given a month's notice and you can ask for repossession to be postponed if you think you can resume payments. Your state or territorial consumer affairs department can help you negotiate this. After repossession, you will be given 21 days to pay the money owing before the goods are sold.

If you have paid off more than three-quarters of the amount owing, the goods can't be repossessed without an order from the credit tribunal (called a commercial tribunal in some states).

If the credit provider has a mortgage over the goods as security for the loan, they are entitled to insist that the goods are insured. However, you have the right to choose your own insurer.

An important right for consumers under the credit laws is the right to have the contract varied in cases of hardship. If you can't keep up the payments because, for example, you are ill or unemployed, you can ask to have the amount of the repayments reduced and the loan extended over a longer time. Let the credit provider know as soon as you experience difficulty and, if they are uncooperative, contact the consumer affairs department in your state for help in negotiating a reduction. You must act quickly, however, to prevent the credit provider taking action against you.

Checking Your Credit Record

If you are refused credit it may be because the credit provider has checked your credit record and found it to be unsatisfactory. The Credit Reference Association of Australia (CRAA) is an organisation that maintains files on peoples' credit worthiness. The information on the files comes from lending institutions.

You can contact the CRAA to get access to your file to check that the information it contains is correct. If it isn't, you can ask the CRAA to change it. If you believe that you have been refused credit unfairly, you can ask the CRAA, the consumer affairs department or the Privacy Committee to investigate.

Credit Cards

Your rights and responsibilities in relation to your credit cards are set out in the conditions which you received when you got the cards. These cover such things as credit charges, credit limits and repayment requirements, and they vary from card to card.

If you lose your card, you must notify the card company within 24 hours – there is a 24-hour emergency number in the phone book. If you don't do this and the card is used, you may have to repay all the missing money. If you do notify them within 24 hours, your liability is limited, even if the card has been used. You don't have to repay any money if the card is used after you have notified the company – unless your PIN number was used. In that case, the company will probably argue that you failed in your responsibility to keep it secure.

If there is a mistake on your card statement, notify the company in writing. Send copies of any relevant credit vouchers or receipts and ask the company to investigate. If you don't think you made the purchase, ask them to send you a copy of the merchant's voucher. If you can't resolve the problem, contact the Banking Ombudsman and/or your consumer affairs department. Doing nothing can lead to your card being cancelled and you being sued for the amount owing.

Legal Action

If you can't pay your debts write to the lender and let them know. Hiding the problem will only make it worse. You could ask for a moratorium on payments, or ask to make lower repayments for a while. If you haven't been able to negotiate a settlement with the credit provider, they will probably send you a letter of demand threatening legal action. If you still don't pay, a summons will be issued telling you to go to court on a certain day.

Even if you owe the money you should go to court on this day and tell the magistrate your circumstances. The court will then try to make an order that you pay by instalments which you can afford. If you have made a reasonable offer to the credit provider and they have rejected it, the court may order that they pay the costs of the court action. Otherwise, you will have to pay court costs as well as the money you owe if the matter gets this far. Obviously, it is important to keep copies of all correspondence with the credit provider.

Sometimes, the court can order 'garnishment', which means that the money you owe can be deducted from your wages or from money you have in the bank. As a last resort, the court can authorise the bailiff to come to your home and seize goods which can be sold to repay the debt.

Just remember that it is never too late to offer to pay the money.

Banking

When you open a bank account, all the usual rules governing contracts for services apply (see Chapter 5). In particular, the bank must exercise reasonable care and skill in its handling of your accounts. If you have a problem and you can't resolve it by talking with or writing to your bank manager, you can contact the Banking Ombudsman. This office has been set up by the Australian Bankers' Association to help resolve disputes where the amount of money involved is less than $100,000.

Before contacting the Banking Ombudsman, you must try to negotiate a settlement with your bank. Once the Ombudsman makes a decision, the bank is bound by that decision but you can seek help elsewhere if you are still not satisfied. The Ombudsman will not, however, interfere with bank policy or with the bank's commercial judgement.

Bankruptcy

Bankruptcy involves having your affairs taken over for a period of time during which most of your assets will be sold to pay your creditors. Some people choose to enter bankruptcy voluntarily: because they haven't got much to lose, their creditors can't pursue them during the period of the bankruptcy; and once it ends they can start afresh with a clean slate.

Bankruptcy should only be undertaken after careful consideration, however, because it may involve restrictions on your life and will have a long-term effect on your credit rating. Never consider bankruptcy until you have sought advice and considered all the alternatives.

Letter to a credit provider seeking extra time to pay

Dear   ,

Re: [loan or account number]

I am writing to inform you of difficulties that I am having with my repayments and to ask that you grant me a temporary moratorium on them.

I am unable to meet my obligations at the present time because [explain your reasons – for example, illness, temporary unemployment etc].

I am confident that I will be able to resume normal payments within [estimated time]. It is for this reason that I am asking for a moratorium rather than a reduction in the amount of each repayment. I understand that the period of my loan will be extended accordingly.

I hope that this request will receive your favourable consideration. I am happy to supply any further information you may require and I look forward to hearing from you shortly.

Yours sincerely,

Letter to a credit provider seeking a reduction in repayment amount

---

Dear   ,

Re: [loan or account number]

I am writing to inform you of difficulties that I am experiencing in keeping up my repayments.

I am unable to keep paying the full amount because [explain reasons – for example, unemployment, illness, increase in number of dependants].

Would you please consider reducing my repayments to [amount] and extending the period of my loan accordingly. Given my reduced income/increased commitments, this is the maximum amount I can afford.

I hope you will consider this request favourably. I will be happy to supply any further information which you may require.

Yours sincerely,

Letter to Department of Consumer Affairs re debt

Dear   ,

Re: [credit provider's name and loan number]

I am writing to ask for your assistance in renegotiating my loan with the above credit provider.

Due to [illness, unemployment or whatever] I am unable to continue repaying my loan at the same rate. I have explained my circumstances to [name of credit provider] but they have refused my request that they reduce the amount of each repayment. Enclosed is a copy of my letter to them and of their reply.

The hardship I am suffering is genuine and I am genuinely trying to meet my commitments. I would be most grateful for your help in this matter.

Yours sincerely,

Letter in reply to a letter of demand

Dear   ,

Re: [loan or account number]

I received your letter dated [date] in which you demand payment of the amount owing under the above loan within 14 days.

Due to [explain circumstances] I am unable to pay this amount within the time specified.

My after- tax income is [amount] from which I must meet the following commitments:[list weekly or monthly commitments, including rent or mortgage payments, rates and utilities, food, insurances, education and travel costs].

I have no savings or other assets which can reasonably be converted into cash to repay my debt to you.

I can afford to pay you weekly/monthly instalments of [amount] each.

Please let me know as soon as possible whether or not you will accept this offer.

Yours sincerely,

Letter to the Credit Reference Association of Australia

Dear Sir or Madam,

Please send me a copy of my credit reference file.
Enclosed is the fee of [amount] (call beforehand to
check this amount – at the time of writing the fee was
$5).

I have lived at the following address/es for the past
three years: [list addresses]

My date of birth is: [date}
My driver's licence number is: [number].

Yours faithfully,

**Letter querying charges on credit card
statement**

Dear Sir or Madam,

Re: [account number]

I have just received a statement of this account which
contains charges for purchases that I have not made.
The charge's reference number is [number], the supplier
[name], the amount [amount] and its date is [date].

I have not bought anything from this supplier. Nor have
I lost my card or given anyone else my number.

Please look into this matter and send me a copy of the
merchant's voucher for this charge. If the purchase was
made by telephone, please send details of the
transaction.

Enclosed is a cheque for my outstanding bill, less the
amount of the disputed transaction. I trust that the
charge will be removed from my account while the
matter is sorted out, so that I do not incur interest.

I look forward to hearing from you soon.

Yours faithfully,

Letter to a bank about unauthorised cashpoint withdrawals

Dear ,

Re: [account number]

Enclosed is a copy of the current statement of the above account. The account shows a withdrawal from the [bank] at [place] on [date]. I did not make this withdrawal [reference number], nor did I lend my card to anyone else.

On the date in question I was elsewhere [details]. I have not lost my card or revealed my PIN number to anyone so I do not know how this transaction could have occurred. I am confident, however, that it is not the result of anything that I have done. It can only be due to some mistake or defect in the procedure for processing credit card debits and withdrawals.

Please investigate this matter and send me a revised statement as soon as possible.

Yours faithfully,

CHAPTER TWELVE

HOLIDAYS AND TRAVEL

Travel agents are service providers and much of the information in Chapter 5 also applies to them also. So are tour operators, hotel proprietors and airlines, bus companies, railways and cruise operators. If something goes wrong with your holiday, you need to decide who is responsible and take the appropriate action. Unfortunately, when mistakes occur with bookings or tours, and hotels don't live up to what you had hoped for, it is not always easy to determine exactly who was at fault.

Travel agents are licensed and they participate in the Travel Compensation Fund so you shouldn't have any trouble obtaining compensation for any losses you incur through the fault of the agent – provided you can prove that it was the agent's fault. An extra precaution, which you can take when choosing an agent, is to check whether or not they are accredited with the major air and sea carriers such as the International Air Transport Association or industry associations such as the Australian Federation of Travel Agents. If you have a dispute with an agent, which you cannot resolve, you can complain to one of these organisations.

Alternatively, you can take legal action through your state consumer claims tribunal or small claims court.

Package Tours

When you buy a package tour, you are entitled to the standard of holiday you were told you were getting, and which you would reasonably expect for the type and price of holiday booked. If first class travel and accommodation were advertised and you find yourself staying at budget hotels, you are entitled to take action against the tour operator.

Tour operators can limit their liability for such matters as currency fluctuations and mistakes in hotel bookings which are beyond their control. The terms and conditions, which they will ask you to sign, will contain all sorts of exemptions. They cannot, however, exempt themselves from the consumer protection laws described in Chapter 5, and you should contact your state consumer affairs department if you have a problem.

Travel advertisements are entitled to be enticing and no-one expects statements such as 'holiday of a lifetime' to be taken seriously. On the other hand, they should not provide information that is false or misleading. The descriptions contained in brochures, which are given to you to persuade you to take particular tours or holidays, form part of your contract with the tour operator. You are entitled to receive what is offered there and to be compensated if you don't.

Air Travel

Airlines know that all sorts of things can go wrong and they take care to cover themselves in the terms and conditions under which they issue their tickets. They generally have the right to cancel or delay flights and to refuse to carry people and goods.

On the other hand, the Trade Practices Commission takes the view that if your flight is confirmed and you are given the impression that you have a firm booking, and you are then off-loaded because the airline has overbooked, they may be guilty of misleading conduct. It is worth complaining, therefore, if it happens.

If the flight is delayed in transit, the airline usually has to cover any reasonable extra living expenses which you might incur.

Travel Insurance

This is a 'must'. You need insurance in case you are forced to cancel your holiday, and to cover your baggage and personal belongings – the liability of airlines and hotels for lost items is usually limited. You should also be covered in case you fall ill. The cost of health care in the country you are visiting may be astronomically high or the standard may be very low – in which case you'll need money to hightail it out of there!

Accommodation

Once your booking is accepted, you are entitled to expect that a room will be available when you get there. If it isn't, you can insist on getting equivalent accommodation elsewhere and on being reimbursed for the cost of arranging it.

You are also entitled to expect that any special requirements which you asked for, and were promised at the time of booking, are available. If you were promised a ground floor room, for example, you are entitled to find it available when you get there.

If you let the manager know as soon as you have any complaints, he or she may be able to do something about it – even to the extent of offering you a discount. If you wait until the end of your stay and then complain, the amount of compensation to which you are entitled may be reduced, because you have a responsibility to minimise your loss.

The hotel's liability for goods which are lost or stolen

while you are there is very limited, unless you have given them to the hotel for safekeeping. To claim compensation for the full value of the goods you have to be able to prove that the hotel, or its staff, were responsible in some way. It is better to have insurance and to give any items of real value to the hotel for safekeeping.

How Much Can You Claim?

Bearing in mind your own responsibilities to minimise your losses by complaining as soon as a problem arises, you can reach an estimate of how much compensation you should claim by calculating:

- the difference between the value of what you got and what you paid for
- something to compensate you for disappointment and loss of enjoyment
- any reasonable expenses you incurred as a result of the service – provider's breach of contract

Letter to a travel agent regarding holiday requirements

Dear   ,

Re: [booking number]

I wish to book a holiday as advertised on page [page number] in the current brochure put out by [tour operator]. I would like to spend [time] in [destination] between [dates]. I note that the advertised price is [amount]. Enclosed is a completed booking form.

Please note that I have some special needs [describe]. I have selected this particular holiday because it offers [features advertised].

Please ensure that I am booked into accommodation that meets the above requirements and confirm in writing that this has been done and that the tour operator is aware of my special needs.

I look forward to hearing from you.

Yours sincerely,

Letter complaining about holiday requirements not met

Dear   ,

Re: [booking number]

I wish to complain about my recent holiday. The holiday was booked with [tour operator] and I spent [time] at [location] for a total cost of [price].

On [date] I wrote to you about my special requirements [detail]. You confirmed that these would be provided in your letter dated [date]. Unfortunately, these requirements were not met. [Describe manner in which you were disappointed].

You undertook to book a holiday in accordance with my instructions, and since the tour operator assures me that they received no such instructions, I must, therefore, hold you responsible for my disappointment.

Please let me know how you propose to settle this matter.

Yours sincerely,

Letter complaining about substandard accommodation

Dear   ,

Re: [booking number]

I have just returned from the above holiday. According to your brochure, it should have comprised [detail].

Unfortunately, the accommodation I received did not live up to these standards. It was unsatisfactory in a number of respects [detail]. I complained immediately, but the problems were not rectified.

The description of the hotel's facilities in your brochure, on the basis of which I booked my holiday, is included in the terms of my contract with you. It was an implied term of this contract that the accommodation would be of a standard that could reasonably be expected for this type and price of holiday.

Since you are in breach of your contract with me I am claiming [amount] in compensation. This is made up of [state how you have arrived at your figure].

Please contact me as soon as possible with your proposal for settling this matter.

Yours sincerely,

Letter rejecting an unacceptable offer

Dear   ,

Re: [booking number]
Thank you for your letter of [date]. Unfortunately, your offer of [amount] in response to my letter dated [date] is not acceptable.

[Describe reasons why the offer is unacceptable].

Unless I receive a more satisfactory proposal within 14 days of today's date, I shall commence legal action to recover the amount owing to me.

Yours sincerely,

Letter complaining about flight delays

Dear   ,

Re: [flight number, date and destination]

I am writing to you about delays I experienced on the above flight.

It was supposed to depart [airport] at [time] but did not leave until [time]. The flight arrived at [destination] at [time]. Your staff explained that the delay was due to [reason].

This delay caused me considerable inconvenience and expense [detail].

It was a term of your contract with me that you would get me to my destination within a reasonable time of the scheduled time of arrival. The delay was due to circumstances within your control, and I believe that I am entitled to compensation.

Please let me have your offer in settlement of this matter as soon as possible.

Yours sincerely,

Letter complaining about lost luggage

Dear Sir/Madam,

Re: [flight number, date and destination]

As a passenger on the above flight, I booked my luggage in at [departure airport] for the flight to [destination]. It did not arrive at [destination].

I reported the loss on arrival and completed the appropriate form. I have not heard from you since.

I understand that since the luggage weighed [weight], I am entitled to [amount] in compensation.

I look forward to hearing from you shortly.

Yours faithfully,

Letter to the Australian Federation of Travel Agents

Dear Sir/Madam,

Re: [name of travel agent]

On [date] I booked a holiday through the above agent. Unfortunately, the holiday was unsatisfactory in a number of respects [describe briefly].

I have attempted to settle the matter with the agent but have been unable to do so. Enclosed are copies of our correspondence in relation to this matter.

I understand that the agent is a member of your Federation. Indeed, before booking my holiday I checked that this was so in order to ensure that I was dealing with a reputable agency. I would be most grateful, therefore, if you would investigate this matter and assist me in resolving it.

I look forward to your reply.

Yours sincerely,

GLOSSARY

ABATE – To reduce something, such as noise. A noise abatement order is an alternative to court action.

AFFIDAVIT – A written statement that its maker (the deponent) swears or affirms is true. Affidavits must contain only facts which the deponent can prove. They are used in court actions instead of statutory declarations.

AFFIRMATION – A statement that something is true. An affirmation can be made instead of an oath if an oath is against a person's religious beliefs.

AGENT – A person who is authorised to act on behalf of another, the principal. An agent's acts bind the principal.

BAILIFF – A court officer who serves documents and carries out court orders.

BANKRUPTCY – A process which allows a debtor's property to be taken over and distributed among his or her creditors.

BONA FIDE – In good faith, honestly.

BREACH OF CONTRACT – One party's refusal or failure to carry out his or her obligations under the contract. Depending on whether it is a condition or a warranty that is breached, the other party may be entitled to damages, or compensation, or to rescind or end the contract.

CAVEAT EMPTOR – 'Let the buyer beware'. The onus

used to be solely on the purchaser to ascertain the quality of goods before buying. This principle has now been eroded by laws aimed at protecting consumers.

CIVIL LAW – Law that deals with relationships between individuals and organisations, for example, law relating to contracts, negligence and nuisance. Civil wrongs give the victim the right to seek compensation or a court order that the wrong be remedied. Criminal wrongs, on the other hand, attract punishment.

COMMON LAW – Law made by judges on a case by case basis. The rule that decisions of judges in higher courts must be followed in later, similar, cases is known as the doctrine of precedent.

CONDITION – An important term in a contract. Breach of a condition allows the other party to rescind, or end, the contract.

CONSIDERATION – The price paid in return for the other party's promise to do something or supply something.

CONTRACT – An agreement that is legally binding. An agreement is legally binding when the parties intend it to be legally binding, and when they each give something in return for the promises of the other.

COOLING-OFF PERIOD – The period of time during which you are entitled to cancel a contract without being penalised.

CREDITOR – The person to whom a debt is owed.

DAMAGES – An amount of money ordered by the court to be paid as compensation in a civil case.

DEFAULT – To fail in some duty.

DEFENDANT – The person against whom a civil court action is brought.

DEPONENT – Person who swears an affidavit.

DUTY OF CARE – The duty to take reasonable care to avoid harming others or their property. Breach of duty of care gives rise to liability for negligence.

ESTIMATE – A provisional guide to the price of services. It is not meant to be binding.

EXCLUSION CLAUSE – A clause in a contract which tries to exclude liability.

FITNESS FOR PURPOSE – Goods must be fit for the purpose for which you bought them. If the seller knew or ought to have known the purpose for which the goods were bought, and they are not fit for that purpose, you are entitled to return them.

GARNISHMENT – A court order requiring a person or body who owes money to a debtor, such as their bank or their employer, to pay it instead to their creditors.

GUARANTEE – A promise that a contractual obligation will be fulfilled. The person making the promise is the guarantor. In relation to consumer contracts, the guarantee is additional to your ordinary rights, not alternative to them.

INJUNCTION – A court order that directs a person to do something or to refrain from doing it. For, example, you can get an injunction to stop someone committing a nuisance.

JUDGEMENT – The decision of the court.

JURISDICTION – The authority of a court to decide the matters brought before it. A court's jurisdiction may be limited to certain kinds of disputes or to certain geographical areas.

LEASE – An agreement between a landlord and a tenant.

MERCHANTABLE QUALITY – The requirement that goods should be of reasonable quality, given the price and type of item involved. They should work properly and last for a reasonable amount of time.

NEGLIGENCE – Failure to take reasonable care to avoid foreseeable harm to others.

NUISANCE – An unreasonable interference with another person's quiet enjoyment of his or her property.

OMBUDSMAN – A public official whose job is to investigate complaints against government agencies and officials.

ONUS OF PROOF – The duty to prove what is alleged.

In a criminal case, the prosecution has the onus of proving that the accused committed the offence as charged.

PLAINTIFF – The person who takes legal action against another in a civil case.

QUOTE (or quotation) – A firm indication of the price of particular services. Intended to be binding (once accepted), the quote may be subject to variations taking into account such matters as the changing cost of materials or any extras or changes requested by the consumer.

STATUTE LAW – Law made by parliament, as opposed to common law.

SUE – To take legal action.

SUMMONS – A document issued by a court letting you know that a court case has started and requiring you to appear to defend the case or to pay money owing to the other party.

TIME IS OF THE ESSENCE – An expression used to indicate that time is a crucial element of a contract. If the goods or services are not delivered on time the consumer, who has made time of the essence of the contract, is entitled to insist on a refund.

TORT – A civil wrong, such as negligence or nuisance.

TRESPASS – The tort of direct interference with the property rights of another person, commonly by going onto his or her property without permission.

WARRANTY – A minor clause in a contract as opposed to a condition (see above). If a warranty is breached, damages can be claimed.

WITHOUT PREJUDICE – A term sometimes used in letters to prevent their being used as an admission of liability or a willingness to settle. What is said in 'without prejudice' correspondence is not usually allowed in evidence in court. You shouldn't use it, therefore, on any letter which you might later need to prove your case.

USEFUL CONTACTS

General
Australian Consumers' Association
57 Carrington Road
Marrickville NSW 2204
(02) 558 0099

Australian Federation of Consumer Organisations
Suites 1 & 2
40 Mort Street
Braddon ACT 2601
(06) 257 6311

Consumer Affairs departments
Federal Bureau of Consumer Affairs
AG Department
National Circuit
Barton ACT 2600
(06) 207 0400

ACT
Consumer Affairs Bureau
Level 3
40 Allara Street
Canberra City ACT 2601
(06) 207 0400

NSW
Department of Business and Consumer Affairs
Head Office
1 Fitzwilliam Street
Parramatta NSW 2150
(02) 895 0111

NT
Consumer Affairs
43 Mitchell Street
Darwin NT 0800
(089) 89 5184

Qld
Consumer Affairs Bureau
State Law Building
50 Anne Street
Brisbane QLD 4000
(07) 239 0416

SA
Department of Public and Consumer Affairs
50 Grenfell Street
Adelaide SA 5000
(08) 226 8211

Tas
Consumer Affairs Council
99 Bathurst Street
Hobart TAS 7000
(002) 34 5155

WA
Department of Consumer Affairs
4th Floor, 251 Hay Street
East Perth WA 6892
(09) 222 0666

Vic
Office of Fair Trading

500 Bourke Street
Melbourne VIC 3000
(03) 602 8123

Legal & Finance
The Banking Ombudsman
PO Box 1999
Carlton VIC 3053
(03) 349 9999
(1800) 337 444

Consumer Advocacy and Finance Counselling
Association
4th Floor
Ross House
247 Flinders Lane
Melbourne VIC
(03) 650 5422

Consumer Credit Legal Service
4th Floor
636 Bourke Street
Melbourne VIC
(03) 670 5088
*give advice over phone,
appointments necessary

Public Interest Advocacy Centre
4th Floor
46 York Street
Sydney NSW 2000
(02) 299 7833

ACT
Legal Aid Office
North Building (ground floor) London Circuit
Canberra ACT 2601
(06) 243 3411

NSW
Legal Aid Commission of NSW
Daking House
11-23 Rawson Place
Sydney NSW 2000
(02) 219 5711

NT
Legal Aid Commission
9-11 Cavanagh Street
Darwin NT 0800
(089) 81 4799

Qld
Legal Aid Office (QLD)
44 Herschel Street
Brisbane QLD 4000
(07) 283 3444

SA
Legal Services Commission
82 Wakefield Street
Adelaide SA 5000
(08) 205 0155

Tas
Australian Legal Aid Commission

123 Collins Street
Hobart TAS 7000
(002) 34 6544

Vic
Legal Aid Commission
of Victoria
179 Queen Street
Melbourne VIC 3000
(03) 607 0234

WA
Legal Aid Commission of WA
105 St George's Terrace
Perth WA 6000
(09) 261 6222

Health
Health Insurance Commission
PO Box 9822
in your capital city.

Travel
Travel Agents – Licensing
500 Bourke Street
Melbourne VIC 3000
(03) 602 8342

Building
Australian Uniform Building Regulations Coordinating
Council
GPO Box 9839
Canberra ACT 2601

(06) 276 2427

Insurance

Life Insurance Complaints Board
PO Box 229 Market St Post Office
Melbourne VIC 3000
(03) 629 7050
(008) 335 405

Claims Review Panel (General Insurance)
Queen Street
Melbourne VIC 3000
(03) 629 4109
(008) 034 496

Ombudsman –
Commonwealth and State
ACT

Australian Capital Territory
Commonwealth Ombudsman
Prudential Building
Cnr University Avenue and London Circuit
Canberra City ACT (06) 276 0111

NT

The Ombudsman
Gallery Level Papalis Centrepoint
Smith Street Mall
Darwin NT 5790
(089) 81 8699

NSW

NSW Ombudsman

3rd Floor
580 George Street
SYDNEY NSW 2000
(02) 286 1000

Commonwealth Ombudsman
9th Level
227 Elizabeth Street (Cnr Bathurst Street)
Sydney NSW 2000
(02) 264 7188

Qld
Ombudsman
25th Floor, Jetset Centre
288 Edward Street
Brisbane QLD 4000
State: (07) 229 5116
Commonwealth: (07) 229 5116

SA
Ombudsman
10th Floor
GRE Building
50 Grenfell Street
Adelaide SA 5000
State: (08) 212 5721
Commonwealth: (08) 231 2861/ [008] 18 2022

Tas
Ombudsman
23 Kirksway Place
Hobart TAS 7000
(GPO Box 960K)

State and Commonwealth (002) 34 9200

Vic
VIC Ombudsman
6th Floor
440 Collins Street
Melbourne VIC 3000
(03) 670 6151

Commonwealth Ombudsman
6th Floor Aldersgate House
405 Collins Street
Melbourne VIC 3000
(03) 614 3911

WA
Ombudsman
18th Floor
St Martins Tower
44 St Georges Terrace
Perth WA 6000
(09) 220 7555

The Banking Ombudsman
PO Box 1999
Carlton VIC 3053
(03) 349 9999
(1800) 337 444

INDEX

Government agencies 83-90
Guarantee 14, 15

Hairdresser 52, 53
Health complaints 61-62
Holiday insurance 99, 100
Holidays 128 *et al.*

'Implied' promises 12-14, 20,
21, 39
Injuries 106-107, 108
Insurance 29, 92-101, 116
    making claims 92-45, 95, 96,
    97
    travel 130
International Air Transport
Association 128

Judicial review 85-86

Language 5, 6, 116
Law Institute 58
Law Society 58, 66
Lawyers 58-61
Lay Observer 59
Letter writing techniques 5-9
'Liability' policy 92
Life Insurance Complaints
Board 93
Loans 115-117, 121,122, 123,
124

Manufacturer's responsibilities
15-16
Master Builders Association 42
'Material Damage' policy 91-92
Materials fit for the purpose 40
Mediations 71
Medical complaints 61-62, 67,
68
Merchantable quality 13, 14,

17, 18, 21, 22, 28, 33
Misleading statements 11-12
Motor vehicle accidents 105-
107, 112, 113, 114
Motor Vehicle Repair Disputes
Committee 31

Negligence 61, 102-103, 108,
109
Neighbourhood Mediation
Centres 71
Neighbours 70
'No Claim' bonus 106
'No Refunds' 15
Noise 72, 73, 78, 79
Nuisance 72

Occupier's liability 103
Ombudsman, Banking 43-44,
    54, 118, 119
    Commonwealth 84, 87
Oral Contract 11
Overcharging 39, 49, 63, 64

Package tours 128-129
Photoprocessor 55
Privacy Committee 117
Professionals 57 *et al*
'Promised Benefits' policy 92
Psychologists 69

Quotes 39, 49

Reasonable Care 103
Receipts 4, 8, 11
Records 3, 5
Refunds 15, 16, 23, 24, 25
Repairs (car) 29, 30, 32, 34, 36,
37, 38, 48
Repossession 116
Returning goods 15

155

Facefacts
A Guide to Cosmetics, Skin & Hair Care

By Alison Haynes

What do we know about the stuff we put on our bodies, especially on our faces and on our hair? Cosmetics (including shampoos and skin care preparations) now have to have their ingredients labelled, but does this make us any wiser? What is the best thing you can do for your skin? How do conditioners work on your hair? Why does bleaching weaken your hair? What do the 'special ingredients' of cosmetics actually do?

Alison Haynes, a CHOICE magazine staff writer, has consulted the experts to research these and other questions and presents her findings in a lively, popular format. Facefacts is a no-nonsense book about beauty choices for the discerning cosmetics purchaser. It gives you all the facts you need to make your own choices about caring for, and buying products for your skin and hair.

Features:

- a broad coverage of all the likely topics in skin care, hair care (including shaving), make-up, animal testing, ingredients labelling, explains the use of terms such as 'hypoallergenic' and 'natural'.
- discusses the importance of sun protection, explains terms such as SPF15
- numerous colourful references to the history of cosmetics use
- gives practical answers to many common skin care dilemma
- illustrated with line illustrations

ISBN: 0 947277 13 7
RRP $18 paperback 224pp
Available from good bookshops and from Choice Books,
57 Carrington Rd, Marrickville NSW 2203.
Telephone: (02) 558 0099 Fax: (02) 558 9341

CHOICE BOOKS

ECOTOURISM
& Nature-based Holidays

By Janet Richardson & the Editors of Choice Books

Ecotourism is the fastest-growing trend in travel all over the world. More and more people want to get close to nature in their leisure time, some in a practical sense as conservation volunteers or scientific field workers. Some just want to relax in a beautiful place and learn more about the wildlife and other local environmental features. But will the ecotourists destroy the environment they seek to enjoy? This book is the first account of ecotourism and nature-based holidays in Australia. It features a directory of nearly 200 tour operators, resorts and other organisations which offer various kinds of natural holidays. The directory not only describes the sorts of experiences available but gives an indication of their 'environmental friendliness'.

About the author:

Janet Richardson has qualifications in Biology and Environmental Management. A conservationist for a number of years, Janet has experience in environmental education. Janet has also had extensive experience in the travel industry as a travel agent and tour operator. In the late 1980s she started *Tread Lightly*, the first ecotourism magazine in Australia (and possibly the world). Janet, a sought-after speaker and ecotourism consultant, combines her publishing and writing activities with the honorary position of President of the Ecotourism Association of Australia.

ISBN 07 3180 423 6
RRP $17 paperback 224pp
Available from good bookshops and from Choice Books,
57 Carrington Rd, Marrickville NSW 2203.
Telephone: (02) 558 0099 Fax: (02) 558 9341

CHOICE BOOKS